DECADES *of* DECEPTION

DECADES *of* DECEPTION

A Novel of Family Intrigue
Based on a true story

PATRICK J. CALLAHAN

ARTEL PUBLISHING LLC

DECADES of DECEPTION

© 2017 by Patrick J. Callahan

Printed in the United States of America

ISBN 978-0-692-03312-8

ARTEL PUBLISHING LLC

807 GREENWOOD DRIVE
SPRING LAKE HEIGHTS, NEW JERSEY
07762

First Printing, 2017

Cover design and layout by Ryan Sanzari

Illustrations by Patrick J. Callahan

www.decadesofdeception.com

www.facebook.com/DecadesofDeception

DEDICATION

To Tina, Clare, and Kate, for their love and patience
during the writing of this book.

Most of all, this work is dedicated to my parents:
Eleanor and Arthur Callahan, who gave me the chance
to become the person I am today.

ACKNOWLEDGMENTS

I'd like to give special thanks to drama critic Rex Reed, who encouraged me to pursue a career in arts and entertainment. We met in summer stock theatre in 1977, and even though I followed a different career, Rex picked up where we left off and offered to write the foreword for this book. "Be more descriptive," he advised. "The sun isn't yellow, it's *saffron.*"

I want to thank Bill Marx, author of *Son of Harpo Speaks!* My loyal interest in the Marx Brothers spurred a thirty-year correspondence with Harpo's late wife, Susan, and son Bill. My family stayed at Susan's Rancho Mirage home in 1997, and it was an unforgettable experience. Bill and I discussed music, his father's life and career, and the ups and downs of our respective childhoods. Bill offered me great understanding and guidance during this time, and kind words for my book jacket.

Many thanks to Steve Fortunato, my agent and marketing guru since 2009. Through his tireless efforts, the book garnered accolades from many of the top literary agents and traditional publishers. Steve knew we had a great story to tell, and he shopped the manuscript to every newspaper, magazine, and publisher in the states. Thanks to Steve, we have a tangible product in the marketplace.

DECADES of DECEPTION is a professionally finished novel because of Ryan Sanzari's talent and hard work. Formatting and design is a painstaking job, and Ryan took each one of my ideas and improved upon them. He arranged the text, incorporated the illustrations and photographs, and designed the front and back covers of the book. I greatly appreciate all of Ryan's tireless efforts.

"Thank you" to my sister-in-law Kate Beckett. Not to be confused with the television detective, Kate is a professional photographer. She produced my author photograph and a myriad of pictures for my website and Facebook page. Thanks to Kate for standing on that shaky chair and taking the aerial shots.

Special appreciation goes to Sharon Casullo for her unending knowledge, organizational skills, and support throughout this process.

Thank you to my two beautiful daughters, Clare and Kate, who make life wonderful and enriching. I love them both as only an adoring, protective Dad can do. Baby Clare experienced the dingy apartments and dark taverns of northern New Jersey, as I searched for clues about my early life. She was strong and resilient, and held my hand from the back seat of the car during those long trips. Kate arrived a year later, and brought the whimsical charm of a little sprite into our lives. Clare and Kate grew into graceful young women with loving, distinctive personalities. I'm a very proud father.

Most of all, true love and immense credit goes to my wife, Tina, for standing beside me on this long, difficult journey. If not for her compassion and encouragement to seek the truth, it's doubtful I would've survived. Tina knew my father for a brief two years, and shared the experience of my life-changing discovery two years later. She has continued to support me throughout the joy and pain of everyday life, and the writing of this book. Tina is my wife, soul mate, and best friend.

FOREWORD

The four basic elements in life necessary for survival are air, water, food, and love. The first three come easy. (Clothes are nice, too, but sometimes you have a much happier time when you take them off.) Love is the inalienable right of every baby from the moment of its first hello, but it is often the hardest to find and mistaken for the one easiest to do without. This is a lie. When love is denied from birth, you are left with a leased identity and a mortgaged heart.

Patrick Callahan is a handsome, sensitive, resourceful, and intelligent New Jersey writer, husband, and father who, on the surface, seems to have it all, but in the remarkable journey that unfolds with candor and persistence in these pages, you will share the heartbreaking saga of how a bewildering series of secrets and lies robbed him of love, and how he spent his life searching for it.

With the questioning innocence of an undaunted child, Patrick knew something was missing from the cradle on. His childhood was filled with mystery and he had vague memories of screams in the night, and a shadow-woman out of a psychological thriller. He had to discover more. So with guile and determination, he vowed to unlock the doors and find out who Patrick Callahan really was, never was, and ought to be. What he learned in the six decades that followed crosses over to the dark side, electrifying with shock value, haunting with the high drama of a mystery by Dashiell Hammett and paced with the breathlessness of a long-distance runner.

Choosing the literary form of a detective novel, Patrick goes to daunting lengths to trace every clue in a bizarre story involving kidnapping, prostitution, alcoholism, payoffs under the table, detours never taken, and criminal plot twists on both sides of the law, played out by a host of unsavory characters, conjured in a patchwork quilt needlepointed from shards of memory so weird some people might label the author delusional.

I know better. I know Patrick Callahan. He lived every salient fact in this remarkable story no matter how sordid it may seem. Cleverly constructed, he peels away each clue like an artichoke without plunging the reader into a gallimaufry of confusion. The reader never knows more (or less) of the narrative at any given time than he does. With subtle brush strokes, Patrick processes the information he uncovers, collates the files he has constructed, and prunes away the clutter while wisely avoiding the kind of pat or sentimental ending that sometimes spoils the impact of other lost-child books.

It starts with an understandable need to close an unfinished chapter in a quest for his identity, but as the facts he uncovers grow more complex, his story becomes more toxic than he ever thought possible. An obsession grows that eventually threatens to damage his ability to move forward. How he manages to put so many disturbing components together no matter how decadent, like a game of Clue, face the facts of his unique story with optimism, and carve a future, make this an unforgettable read. Prepare to lose sleep. You can't put it down.

After years of frustrating dead ends, Patrick Callahan's book *DECADES of DECEPTION*, is finished. He finally knows who he is. A few of the actual locales in his past have been changed, as well as some of the names of the tragic characters who played terrifying roles in his story (many of whom are still alive,) but the facts are unimpeachable. Heroically, he has achieved what so few of us have been able to do by finding inner peace and coming to terms with an unhappy past.

The chronicle of Patrick Callahan's life is unsealed at last. It will inevitably be made into the kind of suspenseful big-screen thriller about which some critic always writes, "This could never happen in real life," but it will be a movie. I will buy the first ticket.

Rex Reed

New York City – June 2015

"The way for a young man to rise is to improve himself every way he can, never suspecting that anybody wishes to hinder him."

Abraham Lincoln

CHAPTER 1

On a scorching summer day, I buried my father.

It was a July afternoon in 1994 when a crowd of mourners gathered around his gravesite at St. Anne's Catholic Cemetery in Spring Lake, New Jersey. My aunts and uncles attended, along with a mixed group of friends and various relatives. There was Aunt Joanie, Aunt Peggy and Uncle Bill, and the rest of the Callahan family. Hermitic Uncle Walter tagged along and buried his head in Aunt Peggy's shoulder as a shrill chorus of cicadas interrupted the solemn air. We huddled under a makeshift tent to avoid the unforgiving sun.

The crowd parted and a priest named Father McGrath emerged. He walked toward the casket carrying a small black Bible in his hands and wrestled to find the correct page. The priest was sick with a cold and stopped to blow his nose in a handkerchief. My emotional aunts mistook the action as a sign of sadness, and they wailed with grief.

I sat under the tent dressed in a dark suit with my wife Tina seated next to me wearing a print dress. Light blonde hair covered her face as she bowed to weep. My father's death left me inconsolable, and I tried to hold myself together, but all efforts were fruitless. There was little solace in the distant group of aunts and uncles who surrounded us.

Father McGrath studied his Bible. He was an ancient priest who counseled my ailing mother many years before over her increased drug use, and I never forgot his cruelty. There was no compassion in Father McGrath's voice. He berated my mother and told her to find God and straighten out her life. I don't think she ever lost God, but the priest offered neither support nor guidance. My mother's condition worsened until we held little hope for her recovery. Sixteen years had passed since her death at fifty-one.

Dressed in a black suit and tab-collared shirt, Father McGrath stiffened and cleared his throat to speak. It signaled the crowd to be silent. I gazed at the American flag-draped coffin set before me, resting on a turf carpet with ropes to lower it into the ground. The stark reality of my father's death caused me to break down. Tina gripped my hand.

"We are here to honor the memory of Arthur Joseph Callahan," began Father McGrath. "He was a loving husband, father, and brother. Arthur served our country during World War II and provided for his family throughout his wife's illness and his son's youth." The priest paused with a wry smile. "Arthur was not a religious man."

A few people chuckled, but not me.

"When I visited Arthur in the hospital to offer him last rites, he said, 'No thanks. I've gotten along just fine without the Catholic Church's help for most of my life. There's no reason to change that now.' I admired his directness."

A trail of soft laughter traveled throughout the gathering as I glared at Father McGrath, and the smile left his face. He trudged on dangerous ground with me, and I was in no mood to hear the priest pass judgment on my father. I motioned for him to move on with the sermon. A rattled Father McGrath got the message and rambled on for another thirty minutes until the speech finally concluded.

I don't think I heard another word.

"I commit the body of our brother, Arthur Joseph Callahan, to the ground. May his soul and the souls of the faithful departed through the mercy of God rest in peace. Ashes to ashes, dust to dust . . ."

The words rang hollow in my ears.

As the priest recited The Lord's Prayer, emptiness and solitude gripped me. It was the stark realization I'd never see my father again, nor talk to him nor seek his advice. The thought of it stopped my heart for a moment, and I slumped in the chair. A year of emotional turmoil and tending to a terminally ill parent had drained me to the core. Only an empty shell remained, sapped of all strength.

Father McGrath closed his Bible to the soft touch of hands on my back. The service had ended. I summoned enough energy to raise my head and acknowledge the people around me, but I had no words.

Workers approached and waited for our departure to lower the casket into the ground, and I couldn't move. Tina gently nudged me to stand and rose from her chair as mourners formed a line to offer their final goodbyes. A gauntlet of hugs and kisses followed with promises to call me in a few weeks, but I didn't expect it. People were just being polite. They said goodbye and hustled away to the comfort of their air-conditioned cars. Even Father McGrath rushed off to avoid any comments I might have about divine disbelief. That's when Aunt Joanie approached wearing a pants suit, earrings, and fluffing her short white hair.

"Come on, Patrick," she said. "It's time to go."

We walked out of the tent and I stopped to gaze at Tina's beautifully sad face.

"That's it," I said. "It's done."

Tina looked into the distance and lamented, "Poor Artie."

Everyone called my father "Artie," including me. For reasons unknown, he alienated me as a child and I wasn't comfortable referring to him as "Dad." It grew into an odd father-and-son relationship, but one I accepted long ago. Artie was more comfortable treating me as a friend than a son. We shopped together in department stores, ate lunch at the diner, and gambled at his beloved racetrack. When Artie got sick, I took the responsibility of caring for him to the end.

Aunt Joanie walked with us past a row of headstones when a loud noise caught our attention. It came from an entourage of blue and white vehicles that thundered up the cemetery road, followed by a green van. A dust cloud mushroomed over the roadway in the stifling July sun, and I recognized the vehicles as Sea Girt Post Office mail trucks. The fleet pulled next to the tent in a military formation and parked. Aunt Peggy and Uncle Bill stood in the center of the road, pointing at the caravan.

"Let's go back," I said.

Tina put her arm in mine and we hastened to the gravesite. Mail truck doors slid open and familiar blue uniformed men jumped out like a postal swat team. They were Artie's co-workers. The mailmen acknowledged us as they passed the casket and filed into the tent.

A group of men in kilts emerged from the green van, dressed in full Scottish plaid regalia. They wore tartan capes, tams, white spats, and daggers tucked into their socks. One man opened the hatchback and the others unloaded a cargo of bagpipes and drums.

Departing mourners stopped along the road to watch this curious spectacle, and a mixture of several conversations filled the air. People couldn't decide whether to stay or jump into their cars and leave, and there was no explanation for the impromptu gathering.

Aunt Joanie took immediate control and motioned for the group to follow her to the tent.

The bagpipers and drummers formed a neat line in front of the casket, and the pipers pumped air into the bellows of their instruments. A noisy collection of various musical notes climbed to the proper pitch as a giant red-haired drum major strode up to the musicians. He wore a high, feathered bonnet and faced the percussionists.

The drum major raised his eagle-crowned mace and commanded absolute silence. Snare drummers began a solemn military-style rhythm punctuated by a steady rat-tat-tat. The bass drummer pounded out a heavy beat with fur-covered sticks, and a low drone emitted from a dozen bellows as the players touched the pipes to their lips. The high-pitched sound of a familiar tune echoed throughout the cemetery.

It was "The Marine Corps Hymn." Artie taught me how to sing the song at the age of five. He was proud of his Marine Corps heritage and delighted in dressing me in his over-sized World War II uniform. I stood on the living room coffee table at every special occasion, and Artie encouraged me to perform the sacred number for houseguests in my high-pitched juvenile voice.

The bagpipers' emotional rendition brought tears to everyone's eyes. The crowd listened while the mailmen stood at attention during the performance. This was a wonderful tribute to their fallen comrade, the perfect end to a sad day.

At the conclusion, the pipe band lowered their instruments and the drum major whirled around to face the casket. He called out an order, and the band members raised their right hands and saluted Artie. Instinctively, I saluted my father, too.

The drummers struck up the beat once again as the band marched away to a reprise of the "Marine Corps Hymn." With a wave, the mailmen climbed into their trucks and drove off to deliver the mail. The music stopped. With military precision, the pipe band loaded their instruments into the green van and the drum major bowed to us. He removed his bonnet, squeezed into the passenger's seat, and the driver sped away. The players had never uttered a word.

The air grew still as two funeral attendants folded the American flag that covered the casket. They formed Old Glory into a perfect triangle and carried her away.

Everyone remained speechless until Jack O'Reilly

spoke my name. He was Artie's old friend and our funeral director for nearly thirty years. I first met him at age ten after my grandparents died just one day apart.

"Patrick, I have something for you," he said.

Mr. O'Reilly presented a memorial display case with the folded American flag from Artie's coffin. He was a tough fellow Marine Corps veteran who'd seen action during World War II, and shared a proud bond with my father that only another Marine could understand.

"*Semper Fi*," said Mr. O'Reilly. "I'll miss Artie's sense of humor."

"Me, too," I replied.

As I accepted the flag, a powerful wind kicked up and blew my hair forward and billowed Tina's dress like a parachute. The air temperature dropped rapidly, and a torrent of black ominous clouds rolled overhead. It was a sign from the heavens heralding Artie's final farewell. Mr. O'Reilly tightened his collar and hurried off with the rest of the crowd as the impending storm gained momentum.

I grabbed Tina's arm and rushed toward the car. She jumped into the passenger's seat just as a heavy rain fell, but I stopped short and looked skyward. Daggers of rainwater struck my face as I cried out Artie's name. The intense driving rain soaked me to the skin, but it was cool and cleansing, and the shower washed away my pain. My eyes closed and a sense of peace warmed my body.

Tina rapped on the car window and shouted for me, but the rain drowned out her voice. I continued to experience my last communication with Artie and couldn't pull away. She yelled my name a second time, and I flipped the door open and dropped into the driver's seat. My tired eyes concentrated on the cemetery workers as they lowered Artie's casket into the ground.

"You're drenched," said Tina.

"The rain felt good," I replied.

Tina wiped the droplets from my brow. "The bagpipers were a wonderful touch. Who sent them?"

"It had to be the mailmen. They played Artie's favorite song." Workers shoveled dirt into the grave, and it gave me a chill.

"Ready to go?" asked Tina. "We have a lot of people coming over for the repast."

I shifted the car into gear and drove off. Massive puddles gathered on the cemetery road, and a steady downpour beat against the windshield as we crept toward the exit. The highway filled with an onslaught of traffic, and I prayed we made it home safe to Spring Lake Heights.

The moment I pulled into our driveway, the rain stopped and a blinding sun reappeared in the sky. It fogged the car windows and heated my soggy clothes until they steamed.

"You should change before everyone gets here," said Tina.

"That's a good idea," I answered. "Shorts and a tee shirt."

My clothing sloshed as we walked up the steps and entered the stifling house. I'd purchased the decades-old ranch last year and made several minor improvements, but air-conditioning wasn't in the budget. As Tina flicked on the paddle fans, I recounted one of my last conversations with Artie.

At the end of June, I sat in Artie's apartment. His once robust frame was skeletal, and his dark hair had turned wispy. A nurse's aide came just once a week to check Artie's vital signs, so I insisted he move in with us on July 1st. I reasoned that his government pension covered the cost of home nursing care and central air conditioning, and we'd be there to take care of him.

"Do you have lots of windows?" asked a worn and defeated Artie. He needed to see the outside world, and I assured him there was a full view. With strong reservations, Artie accepted our offer, but there was one problem; he didn't make it. His condition worsened, and he died on the Fourth of July. I still couldn't believe it.

Tina busied herself setting out trays of food while I changed into dry clothes. I was filling a beer cooler when my aunts and uncles arrived, laughing and talking as they came up the walkway. It was a typical entrance.

The Callahan Clan included six sisters and Uncle Walter, along with their spouses and a few friends thrown into the mix. They grew up in a tightknit Irish Catholic family from Newark, New Jersey, raised during the Great Depression. A tough mother and hard-drinking bartender father formed their distinct personalities.

I referred to my aunts as "The Sisters." They were a raucous bunch with a dark sense of humor that encompassed everything, including death. Each sister became a widow at least once by the age of fifty. This gave rise to Aunt Joanie's comment after Uncle Joe died, "I buried my second husband," she remarked. "I had to . . . he was *dead*, you know!" The Sisters cackled with laughter.

Aunt Joanie was the self-proclaimed spokeswoman and head of the clan. She made the financial decisions, travel plans, and funeral arrangements. The others just obeyed orders. She loved to laugh and tell jokes, but often displayed a cruel side of her personality.

Aunt Peggy became second in charge. Her demeanor was kinder than Aunt Joanie's, but a sarcastic flair still emerged. She attempted to calm her older sister's dark nature with little success and assumed the role of caretaker for Uncle Walter. Shy and childlike, he required constant attention. Artie described him as *not all there*.

Nothing bothered The Sisters, except sickness and emotional issues. I learned that firsthand. It stemmed from an underlying friction between The Sisters and my mother, Eleanor.

Eleanor Callahan was a petite blonde with blue eyes and a wonderful smile, but she suffered from a strange illness and an addiction to painkillers that sent her to the hospital many times. This condition existed as far back as I could remember and caused terrible fights between Eleanor and Artie. They trapped me in the middle, and I blamed myself for Eleanor's illness.

During Eleanor's hospitalizations, Artie dropped me

off to stay with The Sisters and I dreaded those visits. They shuffled me into the corner like a nuisance house-plant and concentrated on their own children. Artie wasn't happy with the arrangement, but he was forced to leave me there while he worked.

The front door opened and interrupted my thoughts. In walked Aunt Peggy, with red cotton candy hair and heavy rouge on her cheeks. The sweet scent of perfume filled my nostrils as she hugged me.

"How are you holding up, kid?" she asked.

"Oh, okay," I replied.

Aunt Peggy embraced Tina as Aunt Joanie entered.

"*Tina-Lina!*" she exclaimed. This was her bombastic nickname for my embarrassed wife. Aunt Joanie gave Tina a big hug and a kiss, then looked at me.

"Hi, Patrick. Do you have a minute to talk?"

"Sure. Let's walk into the den." Tina excused herself while Aunt Joanie followed me. I sensed that something was wrong. She took a combative stance and drilled my face with a cold stare.

"Where is Nana Callahan's handmade quilt?"

"What?"

"The quilt. Where is it?"

"It's at my father's apartment."

"Can you get it?"

"Well, yeah."

"Can you get it *now?*"

"I have a house full of people. Why is it so important?"

"It's a family heirloom, that's what's so *important.*"

"I'll be right back."

I walked to the kitchen and pulled Tina aside. "Aunt Joanie wants Nana Callahan's quilt." There was no time for my wife to react as I tromped off, growing more agitated by the minute.

Pushing my way through the screen door, I spotted my buddy Mike in the yard talking to a few friends. I dangled a set of keys in front of his face and asked if he'd go to Artie's place to retrieve the quilt. Without question, Mike gave me a nod and snatched the keys. The quilt incident disturbed me, and I struggled to think of a reason for my aunt's callous behavior.

I cleaned up after the guests, washed dishes, and performed any menial task to take my mind off the incident. There was noticeable tension in the air, and The Sisters avoided contact with me throughout the day. It only made matters worse. I was dragging out the trash when Mike returned with Nana Callahan's quilt and exchanged it for a bag of garbage. Aunt Joanie acknowledged the quilt's arrival, and I stored it in a bedroom until she was ready to leave.

A few hours passed and our well-fed guests relaxed with cold bottles of beer. It spawned singing, bawdy jokes, and a treasure trove of Callahan family anecdotes, followed by howling laughter. Despite the party atmosphere, my aunts and uncles were still uncomfortable in our home, and I tried not to think about it.

I slipped down the hallway toward the master bath to splash some cold water onto my face. *A couple of more hours,* I thought, *and it'll be over.* Passing by the spare room, I heard Aunt Peggy's voice behind the door.

"Does he know?" she whispered.

"No! Be quiet!" commanded a second voice. It was Aunt Joanie.

I stopped to listen, when one of the other guests appeared and exclaimed, "Hello, Patrick!" My aunts peered through the bedroom doorway like a pair of nervous hens.

"Patrick," announced Aunt Joanie. "We were just talking about you."

"Oh," I replied. They stared at each other during a

moment of uncomfortable silence. *"What* don't I know?"

Aunt Joanie looked to the side and conferred with an imaginary person. She always did that when put under pressure. Her unemotional eyes focused on me. "I haven't told you that I'm moving to Florida in the fall. Aunt Peggy asked me if you heard."

I struggled for an appropriate response and only managed to say, "We must come and visit you."

There was no reaction. Aunt Joanie picked up Nana Callahan's quilt, shot her sister a stern look, and left the room. Aunt Peggy turned with a shrug and trailed behind.

A move to Florida wasn't big news. Three of The Sisters lived in the Sunshine State now, and I expected the rest to follow within the next year. There was more to the conversation than that, and it made me question the true subject matter.

I washed my face and returned to find The Sisters gathering their things to leave. Not surprising after my tenuous discussions with Aunt Joanie. The Sisters masked their obvious discomfort with loud conversation as they moved toward the door with bags of leftovers.

"Goodbye, Patrick," said Aunt Peggy with a sad expression. "If I don't see you before, I'll see you next

March at our annual St. Patrick's Day party."

"I'll be there," I replied. "Nineteen ninety-five will be a better year."

She placed her hand against my face and smiled. "You look like the same kid I knew years ago, with brown hair, blue-green eyes, and that strong cleft in your chin. Nothing's changed, right down to the cowlick on the back of your head." Aunt Peggy chuckled and mussed my hair, as Aunt Joanie approached with the quilt under her arm. Her expression was serious, and Aunt Peggy retreated.

Aunt Joanie pecked me on the cheek and said, "You have Tina now."

The finality of that statement struck me hard. Aunt Joanie turned like a shepherd tending to a flock of sheep and directed The Sisters to exit. The group filtered along the sidewalk to join their surviving husbands in waiting cars.

I leaned against the wall and watched as The Sisters drove away, followed by the rest of our guests. A deep sense of hurt and betrayal burned in my stomach. Dealing with Artie's death was difficult enough without wondering why The Sisters were so distant. Tina stood in the middle of the living room.

"Aunt Joanie made such a scene over that quilt," she

said. "You could've given it to her next week."

"I know, but she *had* to have it now."

"They're angry about something."

"About *what?* We took good care of Artie when he was sick."

"Yes, we did, but they weren't there for their own brother."

Tina was right. Artie suffered from emphysema brought on by a fifty-year smoking habit complicated by war injuries, and The Sisters showed no sympathy. "It's his own fault," declared Aunt Joanie.

That callous accusation brought me back to Artie's last day in the hospital, when he asked if his sisters knew how sick he was. Artie was unaware I'd phoned Aunt Joanie earlier that day and begged The Sisters to visit him one last time. Aunt Joanie was insensitive, as usual. "Call us with the arrangements," she replied. I delivered the cruel decision to Artie, and *damn* was all he said.

The framed American flag stood on the mantel next to a photograph of Artie, Tina, and me at our wedding ceremony. We focused on it for several minutes before Tina walked away crying. Sweaty and exhausted, I dropped to the couch and fell fast asleep in front of the television.

————— ‹◇› ————— .

We woke up late Sunday morning and sat in the living room having our coffee, brooding over one final task; cleaning out Artie's apartment. I dreaded an emotional return and preferred to fantasize that Artie was still living there, waiting for me to bring his supermarket groceries on time. That imaginary notion existed as long as his place remained untouched. I expected Artie to call me with his standard greeting, "What're you doing?" I waited, but the ringer was silent.

"It's time to go," said Tina.

With a snap of the door lock, I walked into the apartment. The air was hot and stuffy, laden with the smell of stale nicotine. Artie lived there for sixteen years after Eleanor died, and I visited him many times. We talked about Eleanor and the good times we shared, never touching on the years of pain and drug addiction that encompassed our lives for so long. Now the vacant dwelling stood as a quiet reminder of my late parents and the short time we spent together. Tina opened the windows to bring in fresh air.

The couch was in disarray with twisted pillows and

blankets. Gauze pads, adhesive tape, and wrappers lay scattered on the carpeting, along with Artie's tossed slippers. It was the scene left by medical personnel as they rushed him to the emergency room for the last time. I picked up Artie's horn-rimmed glasses and tucked them into my pocket. He'd worn the same pair since I was a little kid.

The tiny kitchen remained undisturbed, and I sat at the small round table where Artie spent most of the day. He sipped his coffee there and stared out the window for hours at a time, gazing upon a familiar world that lay beyond his reach. I tried to put myself in Artie's place and focused on an empty bench in the small picnic ground below.

The bench was Artie's favorite spot to read the *Essex County News* and smoke cigarettes, but even that modest pleasure ended when the illness progressed and he became a prisoner of the kitchen table. It broke Artie's spirit and he pined, "This ain't no life."

A few weeks before, Artie sat in the same kitchen chair watching Tina grill steaks for his last Father's Day meal. I hunched over on the bench and looked up to see Artie's mournful face. I could read his thoughts. The end was near and there was nothing we could do to save him.

———— ‹◇› ————

It was the Fourth of July, 1994. Artie lay in a hospital bed talking to me. He paused mid-sentence, drew a deep breath, and exhaled his final words.

"I think I'm going, Pat."

Artie attempted to say something else, but stopped and looked at me with crystal blue eyes. I whispered his name and touched his arm, but there was no response. Artie's eyes faded to gray as the soul left his body.

After thirty-seven years of uncomfortable formality, I leaned forward, kissed my father's forehead, and whispered, "Goodbye, Dad."

I hoped he heard me.

"Artie's belongings are in bags," said Tina as she entered the kitchen. "I packed up his clothing, too."

It was a difficult task for me, and I was thankful that Tina was there to take charge. That left one item on the to-do list. I reached into the upper kitchen cabinet, removed a covered shoebox, and set it on the table. It came from Jack's Army Navy Store in Belmar, where Artie purchased his postal uniforms.

"Artie said everything we need to settle his estate is in

this box."

There was a neat stack of papers inside, with a magazine page torn from *The Postal Record* placed on top. It read: "WHAT TO DO IN CASE OF A RETIRED CARRIER'S DEATH."

"He sure covered his bases," observed Tina.

Artie left a life insurance policy that named me as the beneficiary, along with his wallet, the lease agreement for the apartment, and a handful of old photographs. I sifted through the pictures, and tucked among them was a worn business card with the words:

ARTEL PHOTOGRAPHY STUDIO
140 BROAD STREET
NEWARK, NEW JERSEY

"That was my parents' photography studio back in the 1950's," I explained. "*Artie and Eleanor... Art-El.* It was a little side business they ran."

"What a cute name," remarked Tina.

"Eleanor sold baby portraits door-to-door, and Artie took the photographs in their studio. He said my mother could sell snow to the Eskimos."

Tina laughed. "What happened to the business?"

"They never told me. We lived in a north Jersey town called Redmond back then. After the studio closed, Artie quit his full-time job at the post office and we moved to the Jersey shore town of Bedford near Eleanor's parents in Belmar. My grandmother made friends with the mayor of Sea Girt, and he got Artie a job with the Sea Girt Post Office."

"It's strange that your father quit his job and moved without finding a new position first," remarked Tina.

I nodded in agreement. "For some reason they were in a hurry."

There weren't many photographs in the shoebox, just a few shots of my parents and me in Florida and a handful of Vellum prints from their 1946 wedding. My favorite picture showed a beaming Eleanor and Artie posed together as they cut the wedding cake.

Eleanor's golden wavy hair flowed from beneath her soft veil. Gorgeous light eyes and a white-toothed smile highlighted her small, chiseled features. She wore an exquisite lace wedding dress and a small gold cross around her neck.

I resembled Eleanor more than Artie. She attributed

my pronounced jaw and cleft chin to her estranged father, Robert, who left the family during Eleanor's childhood. My grandmother destroyed every existing photograph of Robert and remarried when Eleanor was nine.

Artie descended from the Spanish Armada that landed in Ireland during the sixteenth century. With strong Black Irish features, a dark pompadour, olive complexion, and perfect teeth, he looked the part of a Latin movie matinée idol. His blue eyes stood out in stark contrast.

The wedding photograph reminded me of Father McGrath's sarcastic accusation that Artie turned his back on the Catholic Church, but my father had good reason for this decision.

When Artie returned home from the war to marry Eleanor, the Catholic Church in Newark refused to sanctify the marriage. The priest reasoned that former altar boy Arthur Callahan hadn't attended mass for three years, even though he was overseas fighting for his country. This explanation didn't move the priest, forcing the young couple to marry in Eleanor's family parish. Artie never forgave the church for turning its back on him. Tina took the photograph from me.

"How sad that your mother died so young."

"Eleanor's golden wavy hair flowed from beneath her soft veil."

"Artie descended from the Spanish Armada that landed in Ireland during the sixteenth century."

"Yes," I said. "I'll never understand what drove her to take those prescription painkillers. Artie said it started with my birth."

"It was unfair of him to say that to you."

"Eleanor was a petite woman, so I assumed she had a complicated delivery and needed the drugs. Maybe that's what Artie meant."

"You can't blame yourself, Patrick. Eleanor's drug addiction devastated Artie, but something else caused her illness."

"I guess we'll never know what that was." The wedding photo was clutched in my hand. "Eleanor and I had a close relationship, but Artie was so critical of me. I thought he hated me."

"Artie didn't hate you," insisted Tina.

"You didn't know him back then. He was a different person. Eleanor's death lifted a weight from Artie's shoulders and his attitude softened toward me. What a shame it took a tragedy to bring us together."

I picked up a color shot of Eleanor, Artie, and me in Miami Beach during the 1960's. "We drove to Florida every winter and my mother's health improved there. After she died, Artie took me on our first car trip alone and something was different. It wasn't just Eleanor's absence, but my new place in her hallowed front passenger's seat. That saddened me. Artie saw this, leaned over and said, 'Wanna go dig her up?' "

"Patrick, that's terrible!" exclaimed Tina.

I laughed. "It was Artie's morbid sense of humor."

With a faint "Goodbye," I closed the door behind me. We walked to the car in silence and climbed in, ready for a much-needed drink at Mulligan's Pub in Sea Girt. It was quiet. Tina gazed at the brick apartment building for the last time with a tear in her eye. I moved closer to her.

"Wanna go dig him up?" I whispered.

She cried. I guess it was a private joke between Artie and me.

"I picked up a color shot of Eleanor, Artie, and me in Miami Beach..."

CHAPTER 2

Mid-October 1996. Two years had passed since Artie's death, and I reassessed my life.

Bedford was my boyhood home; a small rural town located two miles west of the beach, the perfect place to spend a childhood. We moved there in October 1960, and I spent many glorious days playing in cornfields and lush woods. In the afternoons I went to the general store up the block for candy and soda and hung out with a gang of friends, but my true passion was art.

From the time I first held a crayon in my hand, I drew pictures freehand. Coloring books and connect-the-dots weren't necessary to create artwork. I did it on my own. My parents noticed this talent early on, and Eleanor

Eleanor, Artie, and me - 1967

encouraged me to pursue my interest. Adept at drawing people, I created countless portraits of family members, sports figures, and famous people. Movie monsters were a particular favorite, along with popular comic book characters. Second to art came poetry and creative writing, and my teachers encouraged me to follow a career in journalism with a minor in art.

One summer day in 1969, a long-haired neighborhood kid came back from Woodstock with a banged up acoustic guitar strung across his shoulder. We sat on a stump in the woods and he taught me basic chords. I practiced until callouses covered my fingers and taught myself a good repertoire of 1960's music, but that didn't satisfy my burning creativity. I composed original music and transformed my poems into songs, but Artie's only comment was to "stay away from that damned hippie."

My parents had no particular interests in art and music. Eleanor appreciated the talents I possessed, but Artie never understood them. He told me to take the Civil Service test and get a job with the post office, but that wasn't for me. I longed to be a successful artist, songwriter, and musician. Eleanor said my talents came from her estranged father, Robert.

She adored her missing father, and painted a romantic picture of the alcoholic handyman as a gallant figure and accomplished artist who vanished without a trace. Eleanor insisted I bore a striking resemblance to Robert, but there was no photographic evidence to prove it. Just an antique wedding portrait of her parents with Robert's body cut out of the picture. My grandmother did this with a pair of dressmaking shears, and only Robert's right foot remained in the photograph.

Florentyna Schmidt was my grandmother, but family and friends knew her as Flora. She was a tough Polish

"... only Robert's right foot remained in the photograph."

woman who survived the Great Depression and raised Eleanor and her sister on her own.

I loved to visit Grandma Flora's Belmar home, where I was allowed to do anything that made me happy. I planted vegetable gardens in the back yard, drew cartoons on the kitchen table, and ransacked my grandfather's precious workshop without consequence. My reward was a grilled Muenster cheese sandwich and exotic white raisins for dessert.

Wilhelm Schmidt was my grandfather, but I called him Grandpa Willy. He married Flora in 1936 and accepted the role of Eleanor's stepfather. Born in Germany, Grandpa Willy came to this country as a young man and met Flora at a diner in Newark, where she worked as a waitress. After a six-month courtship, the couple married in the St. Stanislaus Polish Catholic Church in Newark. Eleanor and Artie married in the same church ten years later.

Grandpa Willy made crepe pancakes, enjoyed fishing, encouraged me to eat raw clams he harvested at the beach, and taught me basic German phrases. We spent Saturday afternoons at Al's Tavern in Belmar where he drank beer and schnapps, and we arrived home with a smack of Grandma Flora's corn broom. Grandpa Willy showered me with comic books, pet rabbits, and my first Beatles record. In the evening, I nestled against his cushioned form in the easy chair and dozed off watching cartoons.

My grandparents understood how difficult life was in my home. Eleanor fought illness and depression and Artie struggled to keep things from falling apart, so Grandma Flora turned her home into a fabulous playground for a little lost boy. Grandpa Willy offered comic relief to keep me laughing.

Just after my tenth birthday, Grandpa Willy left the house early on a Sunday morning to go fishing and collapsed from a fatal stroke. Eleanor woke me a few hours later to deliver the sad news, and I remembered thinking, *why did Grandpa Willy leave me?* The concept of death was new, and I felt neither grief nor sadness at his passing. The next evening, my traumatized parents took me to O'Reilly's Funeral Home for Grandpa Willy's viewing.

The open casket and sight of my grandfather's waxen face and motionless body shocked me. I preferred to remember Grandpa Willy as the big jolly German fellow who made life bearable. Frightened and shivering, I ran away and flopped into a lobby chair. That's when a fight erupted between The Sisters and another aunt, with Eleanor and Artie huddled on the sidelines.

The argument upset Grandma Flora and she became nauseous. Her knees buckled as I sprang forward and tried to hold her up, but she was too heavy for me. Grandma Flora looked at me with glazed eyes and mumbled, *"Oh, Patty"* . . . We dropped to the floor with a thud and people ran toward us. "Flora's dead!" screamed a woman's voice.

It was December 6, 1966 at six o'clock. My Grandma was sixty-six years old.

The next night, I witnessed both of my grandparents on display at O'Reilly's Funeral Home. The scene was horrifying, and I sat frozen in a chair, detached and devoid of emotion.

Eleanor was inconsolable. Her drug intake increased over the next ten years, and she became a hopeless addict. Artie hoped for a cure and committed her to the Waverly Rehabilitation Clinic in Princeton, New Jersey. He brought me into the clinic through a service entrance for secret visits.

As Eleanor's health declined, Artie vented his frustration on me. My childhood became a living hell. Flora and Willy weren't there to whisk me into their protective arms, so I hid in my room and painted to escape the harsh treatment.

After my sixteenth birthday, Artie sold the house in Bedford and moved us into a Spring Lake Heights apartment. Eleanor's addiction worsened, and she spent most of her time in the hospital. The doctors tried to prepare us for the worst, but I remained in painful denial.

On a cold November morning, Eleanor slipped out the door and visited a local medical center. She hoped to get a prescription for painkillers and arrive back home before we woke, but failed to realize how ill she was. The doctors admitted her, and Eleanor was so ashamed that she refused to contact us.

Artie called every hospital in the area and finally found Eleanor that evening. Her condition was grave, and she lapsed between life and death for the next three weeks.

November 30, 1978. Artie raced to the hospital after experiencing a horrible premonition. He ran into Eleanor's room and a waiting physician told him that his wife was dead.

I arrived home from work that night to see every light

on in the apartment, evidence that something was terribly wrong. I dashed up the stairs with my chest heaving and rushed in to find a stunned Artie standing by the coat closet. "She's gone," he muttered.

My life went into a tailspin after Eleanor died. She was the last person who believed in me, and the prospect of living alone with Artie was unthinkable. Our relationship was sure to disintegrate even further, so I chose to break his grip at the age of twenty-two and move out of the apartment.

All of my meager belongings sat in cardboard boxes and I prepared to leave, when a miraculous thing happened; Artie's attitude changed and he treated me with kindness. In his odd, unspoken way, he was asking me to stay. Artie's plan succeeded, and we lived together for another five years, but he continued to criticize me and kept a tight reign on everything I did. I could only act in the play that Artie was directing.

At twenty-five, my desire for a career in art and music waned. I traded my paintbrush and guitar for a tool belt to apprentice as an electrician and prepared to take the contractor's licensing exam. Artie was skeptical of my ability to run a business, and his lack of confidence drove me to succeed. I got a place of my own and opened Callahan Electric the following year, and built it into a prosperous enterprise.

Artie never said it, but he was proud of me. My father lived long enough to bless my marriage to Tina and visit our first home in Spring Lake Heights, but suffered from poor health in his final years. His death was a critical milestone in my life, but I survived that difficult time with Tina's help.

In February 1996, we welcomed our first child into the world and named her Clare Eleanor. People questioned the old-fashioned middle name, but I didn't need to explain. It honored the legacy of Eleanor and her journey through illness and despair to raise me. I only regretted that Eleanor and Artie didn't live to see their first grandchild.

One Saturday night in late October, Tina marked my fortieth birthday with a surprise party in our basement bar. Friends and neighbors attended, along with Tina's sisters and their husbands, and we celebrated into the early morning hours. Eight-month-old Clare joined the celebration by taking a swim in a huge potato chip bowl, and we thought it was hilarious.

The next day I spent a lazy Sunday afternoon feeling pretty good about myself, and the thought of it made me laugh. Artie never acknowledged my creative talents and referred to my art and musical creations as "pretty good." He allowed his true feelings to slip one time, when I joined the band onstage at my wedding to perform a set of original songs. Afterward I asked Artie if I sounded good. "You always did, Pat," he replied. It was a compliment thirty-five years in the making.

My life was content. I had a loving wife, a beautiful daughter, and a nice home. We owned a successful business that paid the bills and enabled us to vacation in Florida once a year. We always came back from our trips looking tan and feeling relaxed, ready to carry on with everyday life. Everything was perfect except for one question that kept gnawing at me, *why did The Sisters abandon me?*

When Artie was alive, Aunt Peggy kept us on the guest list for her annual St. Patrick's Day party. The invitations ceased right after Artie's death, including the 1995 party that Aunt Peggy mentioned at the repast. The Sisters' continued coolness descended into a blatant shunning.

Aunt Joanie's parting words still rang in my ears: "You have Tina now."

Aunt Elizabeth Black. The name surfaced while I worked in the back yard in the fall of 1996. She was a close friend of Eleanor's from childhood and the un-named person who scuffled with The Sisters at O'Reilly's Funeral Home in 1966. Aunt Elizabeth moved away and disappeared from our lives, and my parents never again spoke of the argument nor Grandma Flora's fatal heart attack. With some hesitation, I called Aunt Peggy and asked for Aunt Elizabeth's address.

"No!" she answered. "I can't give that to you!"

"Why not?" I asked.

"Your Aunt Joanie would have a *fit!* Elizabeth Black hasn't spoken to us in years, and it's not my place to give you her address."

Two days later, an envelope arrived in the mail with no return address. Inside was a scrap of paper with the words, *P.O. Box 55, Saranac Lake, New York, 12983,* penned in Aunt Peggy's neat Catholic School cursive. I accepted the secret gift without question and dashed off a long letter to Aunt Elizabeth. It detailed the loss of my parents, grandparents, and the family alienation. I asked for a possible explanation. A swift five-page reply arrived days later, written on canary yellow stationary. She dated the letter October 29th, 1996, my fortieth birthday, and I wondered if that was intentional.

Fond memories of Eleanor and Artie filled the pages, along with tinges of sadness and remorse. Aunt Elizabeth lost her husband and daughter several years before, and lived alone with nothing but an old movie collection for company. She was glad to hear from me, but sidestepped the subject of my family's estrangement. The letter closed with a phone number, followed by the words, *"Call me."*

CHAPTER 3

It was Sunday morning, November 24, 1996. I awoke early, kissed my sleeping wife and daughter, and walked downstairs to the office. A stack of bills awaited me, but Aunt Elizabeth's letter crowded my thoughts. Three weeks had passed since it arrived in the mail with a phone number, but a deep fear of the unknown prevented me from calling her.

I opened the ragged envelope and reread the contents several times. The words *"Call me"* branded the page. Without thinking, I grabbed the office phone and dialed the number. A woman answered.

"Hi, Aunt Elizabeth? It's Patrick Callahan."

"Oh, my. It's wonderful to hear your voice."

So began our conversation, and my trepidation soon faded. Aunt Elizabeth talked about the past forty years with a vivid memory and described her life in upstate New York. It was a sad story, beginning with the tragic death of her daughter in a mountainside car crash. Husband Charles died of cardiac arrest the following year after a fall down the stairs, leaving her a widow with no children.

Aunt Elizabeth suffered a stroke the year before and a local grocery store delivered food and supplies. The deliveryman remained her only contact with the outside world, and she seemed out of touch with present-day reality.

"Your mother was gorgeous, you know," said Aunt Elizabeth. "What a shame she died so young. I had a matchbook with a lovely blonde model on the cover. She bore a striking resemblance to Eleanor, and I carried that matchbook around in my purse for years. I lost it long ago."

"Something's bothering me," I said. "What happened at the funeral home that night?"

"Well, I didn't want to tell you in a letter," said Aunt Elizabeth. "Joanie flew into a rage at Willy's viewing, then poor Flora collapsed and died. It was all because I asked one simple question, *does he know?*"

"*Know what?*" I asked.

Aunt Elizabeth drew a deep breath and blurted out the words, "You were adopted at birth."

I dropped the phone onto the desk. A freight train of disbelief thundered through my head and my heart pounded. This was a shock beyond belief. Aunt Elizabeth called my name several times in a muffled voice, crying and expressing remorse for telling me the news, but I didn't respond. My hand trembled as I picked up the receiver.

"Why didn't anyone tell me?" I whispered.

"Your parents wanted to keep it a secret," cried Aunt Elizabeth. "It was wrong." She wept hysterically and I tried to calm her. It distracted me from my own sense of panic. Several minutes passed before my aunt composed herself and said, "Maybe you can find your birth mother."

I wasn't interested. Eleanor and Artie took the secret with them in a terrible betrayal, and it was too painful to accept that another woman gave birth to me. The revelation brought forth sudden scores of repressed images in a tidal wave of memories. Locked doors crashed open and flooded my mind with an overload of forgotten vignettes from the past. I jumped from the chair and ran up the basement stairs. Tina stood in the nursery holding Clare as I charged down the hall.

"You're white as a ghost," said Tina. "What happened?"

"I'm adopted!"

Her eyes widened in disbelief. "What are you talking about?"

"Aunt Elizabeth told me I was adopted at birth. My parents aren't my parents."

"My God, Patrick! Why didn't your aunts tell you?"

"I don't know, but they hid the secret for forty years, and so did Eleanor and Artie.

"But why?"

Neither of us had the answer. We talked about the shattering revelation as I nestled Clare in my arms. So many questions arose. *Where did I come from? How did Eleanor and Artie find me? What should I do now?* It hit me. That's why Aunt Peggy asked Aunt Joanie the same cryptic question at Artie's repast, *does he know?* She was referring to my secret adoption.

"Call Aunt Joanie," said Tina.

———⟨◇⟩———

Aunt Joanie wasn't surprised that I learned the truth, and there was plenty of anger in her voice. "Who said you were adopted?" she screamed.

"It doesn't matter. Why did you lie to me?"

"Eleanor *had* to have a baby. Artie didn't care one way or the other, and he knew from the beginning she couldn't have children. Eleanor made a backdoor deal with some attorney and got you."

"Tell me the attorney's name," I said.

"I don't remember, but he was a Jewish guy living on your street in Redmond." Aunt Joanie paused to regain her composure and finished the speech in a cold, practiced style. "I know that you had a tough childhood, Patrick. If anybody deserves to be a drunk and a drug addict, it's you. Your parents sacrificed everything to keep you safe because they loved you."

"It's a pity you don't feel the same," I countered.

"I knew you'd find out sooner or later," said the voice of Aunt Peggy. "Artie called us to the house late one night to see the new baby, and we swore not to ask where you came from. Eleanor brought you home, and Artie was angry at first, but over time you became his son."

That evening, I walked around in a fog of disbelief. Eleanor adopted me without telling Artie, and his lack of involvement set the stage for our strained relationship. Aunt Joanie's unsympathetic nature made matters even worse. My family ties ended with Artie's death, but no one bothered to tell me.

Tina suggested we go to Mulligan's Pub for a distraction. It was better than watching me pace around the house wallowing in self-pity, but the wound was still fresh and I had no interest in socializing. I struggled to rationalize my parents' decision to hide the adoption and rolled the information around in my head. Tina knew it was driving me crazy and insisted that we go out to be around other people. It would take my mind off the news. Reluctantly, I tucked Clare into her car seat and we were off.

Mulligan's Pub was my favorite place to relax with friends after work. Sometimes Artie slipped in unnoticed to display his mock disapproval of my presence at the bar. He'd have a soda, talk about the day's events, and try to tuck a roll of cash into my hand.

The place was crowded, and tall ex-ballplayer Hughie the bartender set two beers down on the bar. "Hi-ya, Paddy," he said. "Somebody's trying to get your attention."

Judy Forman waved from the far side of the room. She and her husband Sam recently moved from Redmond to Sea Girt, and became proud regulars at Mulligan's Pub. We squeezed through the crowd and joined them.

"Hello, Patrick," said Judy. "Clare looks like a little Irish doll."

We clinked our beer glasses together and said, "Cheers." Tina chatted with the Formans while I sipped my drink and thought about Redmond. Eleanor and Artie never referred to the town again after our move to the Jersey shore. They erased that time period from our lives and it faded from my memory, replaced by youthful recollections of Bedford.

"Let's get a table," said Tina.

"Go ahead," I replied. "I'll join you in a minute. There's something I want to ask Judy."

Tina said goodbye to the Formans and disappeared into the crowd with Clare. Judy looked at me with tepid curiosity as I whispered, "I received some disturbing news today. My parents adopted me at birth in Redmond."

"Really?" she remarked. "That's incredible. Who told you?"

"My estranged aunt. She said a Jewish lawyer from Redmond arranged the adoption."

"Howard Saltzman!" announced Judy. "He's the seediest adoption attorney in Redmond!" My mouth dropped open. "Saltzman is still in business, just check the *Yellow Pages*."

Words escaped me as Hughie yelled across the room, "Hey, Tina wants to order."

Tina and Clare sat at a booth with raised menus as a signal. I excused myself and slid into the bench seat across from them. "I've got an attorney's name: *Howard Saltzman*, and he's still practicing in Redmond. Can you believe that?" I took a huge swallow of beer and almost choked. "I'll look him up tomorrow."

"Maybe you should call Len first," suggested Tina. "He can advise you what to do. I think adoption records are confidential."

She was referring to our attorney. It might be a wise choice to confer with him before I jumped into anything.

"Good idea," I replied.

I ate my dinner like a zombie while Tina fed Clare.

A gray haze clouded my vision, and fast-moving scenes flashed before my eyes. *A strange lady in dark glasses calls my name. I'm scalded in a hot shower and fall down a flight of rickety wooden stairs. I take a ride in a police car.*

My fork dropped to the plate with a clang and the fog lifted. Tina looked at me like I was a raving lunatic, and Clare's cherubic mouth dripped baby food.

"What's the matter?" asked Tina.

Before I could answer, another scene appeared. *I'm four years old and refuse to take a warm shower. I want it cold. Eleanor turns on the cold water tap.*

"Patrick!" said Tina. "What's wrong?"

The scene vanished and my head snapped back. "The scalding incident," I replied.

Tina knew the story. When I was a toddler, Nana Callahan fell asleep babysitting me. I crawled into the tub, turned on the hot shower, and burned myself. That's what my parents told me.

There was a serious look on Tina's face. "I haven't said anything until now, but I never believed that explanation."

Her statement matched a secret doubt I buried for

many years. "It does seem far-fetched," I said. "Why am I seeing these things?"

Tina thought for a second. "You're traumatized, Patrick, and it's bringing back long-forgotten memories. Maybe it's time to look at it from another perspective. You have to forget everything your parents told you and start over."

CHAPTER 4

Howard R. Saltzman – Attorney At Law.

The name jumped out from the *Essex County Yellow Pages*. After forty years, he retained a practice at 1000 Main Street in Redmond. If Saltzman lived on my parent's street in 1956, he probably arranged the adoption. I tore the page from the library phone book and stuffed it into my coat pocket. The Sisters *had* to know his name. I took the soft approach and called Aunt Peggy for confirmation.

"Is Howard Saltzman the attorney?" I asked.

"*Howard Saltzman*," exclaimed Aunt Peggy. "Where did you get that name?"

"From someone living in Redmond. Was he the one?"

"Patrick, there's no sense in bringing up the past. Go

on with your life, you're happy now. You have a lovely wife and a beautiful daughter. Be satisfied with that."

"Aunt Peggy, I have to get the facts. Everyone lied to me for forty years and it has to stop *now*."

She took a long pause before answering. "Howard Saltzman was an attorney who lived across the street from your parents on Hillside Avenue in Redmond. He found a baby and Eleanor brought you home at five days old. I'm not sure what happened, but your parents abandoned the house in the dead of night two years later and fled to Bedford. That's all I know."

Landis Armstrong was my attorney and Tina's employer, but most people called him Len. He joined me for an occasional pint of lager at Mulligan's Pub.

It was eleven o'clock on a Monday morning when I said hello to the receptionist and breezed into Len's private office with briefcase in hand. This wasn't unusual, and Len barely looked up from his work.

"I have something crazy to tell you, Len. My parents adopted me at birth."

For once, my opening line caught Len's attention like a three-alarm fire. He threw his glasses onto the desk and exclaimed, "Wow, that's a bombshell. My goodness, how are you handling the news?"

"I'm taking it one day at a time."

Len settled back in his chair and studied me. "The implications are mind-boggling."

I handed him Saltzman's *Yellow Page* ad circled in red pen. "This is the adoption attorney. I want to find my birth mother, and I'm hoping you can help me."

"Howard Saltzman," said Len. "Let's look him up in the *Lawyers Diary*." He whipped around and grabbed a red hardbound book from the shelf and flipped through the pages. "Here he is. Saltzman's an old-timer; entered the bar in 1951." Len looked at me with a half-smile. "Let's give him a call." He switched on the speakerphone and dialed Saltzman's phone number. After four rings, an answering machine picked up.

"*You have reached the law offices of Howard Saltzman,*" said a woman's voice. "*Please leave a message.*"

"Hello, Mr. Saltzman," began Len. "My name is Landis Armstrong. I'm an attorney down the shore, and I'm sitting with Patrick Callahan. We'd like to know if you performed the legal work for his adoption. Please call me to discuss the matter." Len left his phone number and folded his hands together.

"All we can do now is wait," he said.

Artie's shoebox gathered dust on the living room book-shelf for over two years. Each day I passed the tattered cardboard container and reminded myself to sort through it. There might be a hidden adoption reference I didn't notice before. It was a task I'd avoided since leaving Art-ie's apartment on that distant Sunday morning.

Without thinking, I snapped up the shoebox on a Sat-urday afternoon. Tina was shopping with her sisters, and Clare played with her doll collection on the couch. I eased down next to her, opened the lid, and picked out my par-ents' wedding photograph.

"Mom-Mom and Pop-Pop!" said Clare. She pointed at the photo and repeated the phrase. It brought a smile to my face.

Eleanor and Artie 's birth certificates, social security cards, and final driver's licenses were intact. A yellowed birth certificate lay at the bottom of the box with the heading, *Patrick Joseph Callahan*. I'd seen the document many times and noticed nothing unusual about it. This time I looked closer and realized the registrar dated the certificate January, 21, 1958, almost fifteen months *after* my birth. It was the discrepancy I hoped for.

On a cold winter morning, I took my birth certificate and drove northbound on the Garden State Parkway toward Essex County. An hour and twenty minutes later, I pulled my truck into the Redmond Municipal parking lot, and walked into the Vital Registrar's Office. The woman behind the desk ignored me.

"Excuse me," I said.

She looked up. "Can I help you?"

"I'd like to see my original birth certificate."

The registrar got up and walked over as I placed my copy on the counter.

"My name is Patrick Joseph Callahan. This is a copy of the original document, but I want to see the *original*."

She furrowed her eyebrows and went to a large filing cabinet. With the deftness of a town employee, the registrar flipped through the section marked "C" and found the original birth certificate. She returned and slapped it onto the counter, "It's the same thing."

Both copies matched. *Eleanor and Arthur Joseph Callahan are the natural parents of Patrick Joseph Callahan, born on October 29,th 1956 in Redmond General*

Hospital. It was issued on January 21, 1958.

"Why was my birth certificate issued more than a year after my birth?" I asked.

"I don't know," she replied. "Maybe your parents lost the original and this is a re-issue."

"It doesn't say I'm adopted."

The registrar gave me an annoyed look and marched back to the filing cabinet. She rummaged through the "C" section once again.

"A small index card is stapled to *all* amended birth certificates, indicating there's a sealed adoption filed in Trenton. There's no index card attached to the birth certificate or laying loose in the drawer. You aren't adopted."

She raised the original certificate and we saw two Dracula-like puncture marks in the corner. Staple marks. With a twisted smile, the registrar said, "Your parents did a thorough job."

I barreled through the door of town hall and hustled down the steps to the pavement. A dark curtain covered my eyes, and I stopped in the middle of the sidewalk. It was another flashback. *I'm two-years-old and Eleanor is crying on the telephone. A woman threatens to kidnap her baby.*

Eleanor told me the story long ago and repeated it just before her death. Artie gave the same account in his dying days and described the stranger as *just some nut*. These visions came to me with more frequency since my conversation with Aunt Elizabeth, *but what did they mean?*

On Saturday morning, December 14, 1996, I called Howard Saltzman. Two weeks had passed since Len Armstrong left him a voicemail and there was no response. As expected, the answering machine picked up.

"Hello, Mr. Saltzman. My name is Patrick Callahan. My attorney, Len Armstrong, left you a message a couple of weeks ago." There was a click.

"*Patrick Callahan!*" proclaimed a booming voice. "I haven't heard that name in thirty-nine years!"

"Mr. Saltzman?"

"Yes. How are you?"

"Well, I've been better. I just found out I was adopted."

"Oh, that's a shame. I advised your parents to tell you the truth when you were old enough to understand. How are they?"

"They're both gone."

"Sorry, I didn't know."

"Did you get my lawyer's phone message two weeks ago?"

"No, I didn't. It's possible that my secretary erased it by accident, but I can't be sure. You know, adoption is a noble cause, but people should be honest about it. I have five adopted children of my own and we raised them with great love. So, which of your parents died first?"

"Eleanor, in 1978. Artie passed away sixteen years later."

"That's odd. Eleanor was a healthy and vivacious woman when I knew her, and Artie was ill with respiratory problems. Eleanor must've gotten ill after they moved from Redmond."

"Why *did* we move, Mr. Saltzman?"

"I'm not sure. Your parents left in the middle of the night and we never saw them again. Elsie was my wife back then, and we were best friends with Eleanor and Artie. Your parents even offered their home as campaign headquarters when I ran for city council president with the Fine Young Democrats of 1956. Frankly, I was rather dismayed that they disappeared so suddenly."

"What year was that?"

"It had to be around 1958."

"I'm having strange visions of falling down stairs and being scalded in a hot shower. I see the face of a mysterious lady, and remember Eleanor and Artie talking about a woman who threatened to kidnap me. Do you know anything about those incidents?"

"Why, no," replied Saltzman. "This is the first I'm hearing of it."

"They must mean something," I said. "So here's the most important question: did you handle my adoption?"

Saltzman bristled. "I didn't *handle* your adoption; I provided the legal work. You make it sound as if I did something illegal, like *baby-selling!*

I'd struck a sensitive chord with the aged attorney, and he knew it. Mr. Saltzman recovered quickly, and continued in a calm voice.

"Patrick, allow me to explain. After ten childless years of marriage, Eleanor and Artie applied to Catholic Charities and the State of New Jersey to adopt a child, but both agencies turned them down. It was because of Artie's nervous condition from the war. From that point on, Artie gave up on the notion of adopting a baby. Eleanor asked me for help, and I located a woman willing to relinquish her unborn child."

"What was her name?"

"Oh, I don't remember. That was forty years ago."

"You must have my adoption record."

He thought for a moment. "I usually keep all marriage, divorce, and adoption records in my basement archives and I'd have to search for it. Eleanor and Artie were close friends, so it's the least I could do for you. I'm sorry that things worked out this way, my boy. I guess it was some misguided attempt on their part to protect you.

"There is one interesting point; a woman named *Lana* called my office two weeks ago and asked about your adoption. She knew that you went with the Callahans, but I refused to divulge any information about them and hung up on her. She was rather pushy."

"Do you know the exact date she called?"

"Let me examine my call log." I heard the rustling of papers. "Here it is. November 25th."

"That's the day after I got the news."

Saltzman didn't comment about the coincidence. "Patrick, I have to go, but I'll call you when I find your adoption file."

The hollow buzz of a dial tone reverberated in my ear.

CHAPTER 5

The call was brief on Wednesday morning. "Come to my office Friday night at eight o'clock and I'll give you your adoption papers," said Saltzman. "By the way, your mother's name is Doris."

It was a cold and clear December evening, and every star was visible in the crisp night sky. My warm breath rose into the atmosphere as I started the car and shook off the bitter chill, eager to start my journey to Redmond.

Christmas was just a few days away, and Howard Saltzman promised to give me an early present before the holidays. I prepared myself to be surprised, grateful, or disappointed. Only the aged attorney knew which category might fit the occasion.

Tina stepped outside carrying Clare, as I rose from the driver's seat. She paused and held my hand as our eyes met.

"Patrick, I hope you get the answers you're looking for."

I looked up at the brightest star that pierced the darkened heavens and said, "I think Eleanor and Artie want that now."

The name "Doris" played in my mind during the drive. I prayed she was a misguided young woman, forced by circumstance to give up her newborn baby. Perhaps the pain of relinquishing a child proved too difficult to bear, and she'd entered into a life of quiet anonymity. I'd been given a second chance for a mother-and-son relationship and swore to work harder at it this time around.

An old two-story wood frame structure stood at 1000 Main Street in Redmond. A hand-painted sign listed "Dr. Ortiz" on the ground level and "Howard Saltzman - Attorney-At- Law" on the second floor. There was no elevator, just an old stairway.

A steep climb up the flight of noisy wooden stairs brought back that childhood fall. It was so real I lost my senses and grabbed the handrail to prevent an actual recurrence. Tina clutched my arm and I leaned against her until the vision subsided. Clare remained pressed between us.

"Patrick, what happened?" cried Tina.

"The fall. I relived it again."

We stepped into a dim-lit hallway and the door at the end opened with an eerie creak. The reception area smelled musty, as if no one had opened a window for the last century. There was a secretarial desk in the middle of the room piled high with papers and work files. Wooden shelving overflowed with legal tomes and classic literature. Our host was a well-read man.

A gentleman's deep voice echoed from the inner office. We stood breathless and surveyed a room filled with framed certificates and awards, and I read each one of them in a state of nervous anticipation. Tina moved closer as the clunk of a telephone handset caught our attention. A shadowy figure appeared in the doorway and spoke. "Please, come in."

Howard Saltzman stood tall and heavyset in a dark suit with wavy white hair that curled behind his ears. He studied us with a pleasant face, complimented by a generous nose and sad eyes that twinkled as he spoke. "Patrick, it's good to see you again." Saltzman shook my hand with a powerful grip.

"It's nice to meet you, Mr. Saltzman. You have a strong handshake."

He laughed. "I used to be a ballplayer back in my salad days. You must be Mrs. Callahan."

"Please, call me Tina," she answered. "This is our daughter, Clare."

Saltzman bowed and smiled at Clare. "She's beautiful." The attorney stood and motioned with his right hand. "Make yourselves comfortable."

The room was dark except for a lone gooseneck lamp that threw a sphere of light onto the desk. We settled in two chairs and Saltzman took a long look at me. "It's been many years. You were just a little Irish pug when I last saw you." He grinned. "Eleanor and Artie lived across the street from us on Hillside Avenue. Eleanor longed for a child of her own, and an opportunity presented itself."

"I'm anxious to hear about that," I said.

"Then let's get started," replied Saltzman. He donned a pair of heavy reading glasses with taped-up frames and reached into a worn legal brief. Several onion-skinned typewritten pages crackled in Saltzman's hands as he offered me a set. It was like holding the Declaration of Independence.

"Patrick, before you are four documents; an Adoption Complaint, a Child Welfare Report, a Final Judgment of Adoption, and your original birth certificate. The Adoption Complaint contains your birth mother's biography and the events leading up to your adoption by the Callahans. Please follow along while I read through this document.

"You are the natural child of Doris Sochek. She's described as a sad-looking individual with light brown hair, green eyes, and a large build, standing at six-foot-tall.

"Doris gave birth to many children by several different men and lied to her husband Karl, claiming he fathered those children. She demanded hush money from your actual birth father, a married man named William Van Winkle.

"Karl was furious when he found out and confronted Doris. She admitted it was Van Winkle's baby, and revealed that Karl was not the father of the other Sochek children. Karl left Doris and disappeared.

"Doris was destitute and moved into her sister's apartment at 15 Trafalgar Drive in the Newark Projects. It was a low income housing development for the underprivileged." Saltzman lowered his head and peered over his glasses. "The city tore it down in the 1970's."

I listened in spellbound silence as Saltzman continued.

"Doris secured employment at the Newark Public Library, and told co-worker Connie Taylor that she wished to give up her unborn child for adoption. Connie and her husband John were close friends of Eleanor and Artie Callahan. Connie told Eleanor about the offer, and Eleanor asked this attorney to act as the confidential intermediary."

"I remember Connie Taylor from my childhood," I said. "So she set this up."

Saltzman nodded and continued. "Six months into the pregnancy, Doris backed out of the agreement. I had the unpleasant duty of telling Eleanor that the deal was off, and the news devastated her. Desperate for a child, Eleanor charmed Connie into giving her the name and address of the expectant mother.

"Eleanor went to Doris' tenement apartment and persuaded her to reconsider. She visited Doris several times and brought her money and clothing, and the prospective mother agreed to the adoption." Saltzman removed his glasses and looked at me. "Eleanor made a mistake by revealing her identity to the biological mother. The adoption was private and no names were to be given, but it was too late for that."

"She was desperate for a baby," interjected Tina. "You can't blame her."

"I'm not blaming anyone, but you're supposed to listen to your attorney. You may not be aware of this, but Eleanor endured a full hysterectomy at age sixteen and was unable to conceive a child. Artie knew that from the beginning, and gave up on the notion of adoption when he didn't qualify. Eleanor remained undaunted and continued to search for a baby."

The news of Eleanor's hysterectomy crushed me, and Saltzman paused before he continued reading the report.

"On November 2nd, Eleanor and a friend met Doris outside Redmond General Hospital. They gave her a ride to the bus terminal and Eleanor took you home.

"The biographical section of the report states that Doris Sochek was born in Mountainside, New Jersey on August 1st, 1929. She was one of three children." Saltzman paused, choosing to paraphrase the next section. "Doris' father abused her."

The information made me nauseous, and I wondered if Doris ever recovered from that dreadful desecration. My heart sank with the knowledge, and the notion of an innocent, misguided young mother faded away. Saltzman rose and paced around the desk with the documents in his hand.

"Next we have the Child Welfare Report, and I quote, 'Mrs. Callahan is of average height and has a slight build. She has a fair complexion, long blonde hair, and blue eyes. She is a soft-spoken, well-poised person of good health. Mrs. Callahan is well qualified to care for the child.' "

He looked at me. "The Callahans provided an adequate home for you, and paid $340 for Doris Sochek's medical bills and hospital stay. I received $120 for expenses.

"The remainder of the report details Eleanor and Artie's biographies, work history, and that sort of thing. They lived in a quaint Cape Cod at 3 Hillside Avenue in Redmond, and provided a loving home for the child." Saltzman sighed. "That was the Eleanor and Artie I'll always remember."

"I wish I had known that side of them," I said.

Howard Saltzman sat down with a single sheet of onion-skinned paper in his hand. "This is the one-page Judgment of Adoption, which declares that the relationship between the child and his natural parents shall be terminated." He picked up one final document. "Here is your original birth certificate."

I lifted my copy of the colorized certificate with great care. It was a work of art, with the soft image of an infant boy floating across a light blue sky laced with velvety clouds.

Redmond General Hospital towered in the background, and a tiny handprint and footprint graced the bottom corner. The health registrar stamped the document with a seal and typed my original birth name, "Patrick Joseph Sochek." It was the name of a stranger who never existed.

Saltzman referred to me as *a little Irish pug*, but there was no evidence of Celtic roots on either parental side. It was a curious observation on his part.

"Why are both birth certificates dated January 21st, 1958?" I asked.

"It took that long to file the petition," explained Saltzman. "Well, I think that's everything."

"It's an overwhelming story," I remarked. "So where is Doris Sochek now?"

A serious expression covered Howard Saltzman's face. "You'll never find her... the trail is cold."

He made that statement with great conviction, and I wondered why there was such certainty in his voice.

"Your birth mother was a very troubled woman, bordering on psychotic. She showed up at the courthouse and objected to the final decree of adoption. I physically pushed her out the door to avoid ruining many months of hard work."

The word *psychotic* dominated my thoughts. "Over the phone, you said that my parents disappeared in the dead of night sometime in 1958. We moved to Bedford, New Jersey in 1960, so that leaves a two-year gap in time. Where did we live during that period?"

Saltzman looked surprised. "I have no idea."

All the loose ends in this story perplexed me, and I grappled with more questions for Howard Saltzman. The best I came up with was, "Tell me about the woman named Lana."

"Our conversation was brief and she knew that you went with the Callahans," said Saltzman. "I gave her no information about your family and hung up. That's all I can tell you." He switched off the desk lamp and walked out from behind his desk. "That's everything, Patrick. Good luck."

The night air was cold. I put my arm around Tina as she wrapped Clare in a blanket and hurried to the car. We sat motionless while the heat kicked in.

"What do you think?" I asked.

Tina shook her head. "It's all so disturbing."

"That was the Eleanor and Artie I'll always remember."

CHAPTER 6

Doris Sochek had vanished, and William Van Winkle slipped into obscurity. That left just one person with possible answers: Connie Taylor.

Connie and John Taylor moved to Toms River twenty-five years ago. After Eleanor died, Artie drove to John's house several times but refused to knock on the door. It was strange behavior for a boyhood buddy from Newark.

John and Artie enlisted in the Marine Corps together, suffered explosive injuries on Guadalcanal, and arrived home on the same hospital ship in 1945. John Taylor died and Artie never mentioned his name again.

"Why don't you drive to Connie's house?" suggested Tina. "Only this time, go up to the door."

I parked my red Callahan Electric truck in front of Connie Taylor's modest ranch. Soggy yellow newspapers covered the porch, still rolled in plastic. I reached the steps and someone studied me through the window curtains. A deadbolt clicked as the door opened halfway, and a slight woman with pasty skin and white hair appeared. Two fingers removed a long thin cigarette from her lips and blew a puff of smoke my way. I choked from the stench.

"Can I help you?" said a rough voice.

"Are you Connie Taylor?"

"Who wants to know?"

"Patrick Callahan."

"Eleanor and Artie's son? Please, come in."

The house reminded me of Artie's apartment. It was dark, stale, and smoky. Rust-colored curtains concealed crusted windows, and we stood on a brown shag rug.

"It's been a long time," said Connie. "I heard that Artie died."

"He had emphysema," I replied.

Connie took a drag from her cigarette and let out a cough. "I wish I could quit smoking, but at my age it doesn't matter anyway. John died of cancer ten years ago and so did my son and daughter. I'm alone now." We walked into Connie's kitchen and she mentioned reading Eleanor's obituary several years before. "She was my best friend. It's a shame we drifted apart, but things happen."

"What things happened?" I asked.

She tilted her head to the side. "Oh, you know, children came along, then your parents moved down the shore. John and I stayed in Redmond another fifteen years before we came here, and by that time we lost touch with Eleanor and Artie. I'll make some coffee."

Connie filled a coffee pot at the kitchen sink while I took a seat at the table. I dropped a copy of my adoption record onto the plastic tablecloth, and Connie observed me through narrow eyes.

"Did you know that Eleanor and Artie adopted me?" I asked.

"Yes," replied Connie. "Because I'm your godmother."

The admission stunned me. "I never knew that, and they didn't tell me I was adopted."

"Your parents didn't tell you a lot of things," said Connie. "What do you have there?"

"These are my adoption papers. You're listed as the contact person between my birth mother and Eleanor."

"That's a lie!" shouted Connie.

She snapped the faucet handle down and plumbing pipes rattled inside the wall. Connie splashed water into the machine and snapped on the switch. The red indicator light on the coffee maker matched the fire in her cheeks. She lit another cigarette and snapped up the report to read it.

"I didn't work with anybody named Doris Sochek at the Newark Public Library. Who gave all this personal information about me?"

"Eleanor and Artie," I answered.

Connie glared at me. "It's all made up! They used me to create this story. I had nothing to do with your adoption." She flipped the report at me and clung to the chair gasping for air. I jumped up to help her, but Connie extended a hand to stop me. "Sit!" she commanded. Connie stood there for several minutes regaining her composure, then filled two coffee cups with feeble hands.

"Why would my parents lie?" I asked. "You were good friends. It makes perfect sense that you helped them with the adoption."

Connie's eyes welled with tears. "That's just it. I had no involvement. John and I knew Eleanor planned to adopt, but she was secretive about it. Then I heard there was trouble, but no one knew what happened." She wiped her eyes and eased into a chair. "What else do you want to know?"

"Tell me about your relationship with my parents."

"They were wonderful people," said Connie with a smile. "Eleanor was so beautiful she could have been a movie star, and Artie was dashing, with dark hair and blue eyes. They were successful baby photographers who lived the high life and moved up the hill."

"That's where they met Elsie and Howard Saltzman."

Connie pointed a crooked finger at me. "Exactly. They were the ones who set up your adoption, not me. The Saltzmans convinced your parents to use my name because we were friends." She took a sip of coffee. "Is Howard Saltzman still around?"

"Yes. He gave me the adoption file."

"Saltzman knows the real contact person."

"He says it's you."

"Bull!" she yelled. An agitated Connie inhaled on her cigarette and struggled through a ten minute coughing fit. I waited patiently as she smothered her face in tissues and took a shaky sip of coffee to quell the attack. I'd witnessed similar events many times at Artie's kitchen table.

"I do have something else to tell you," said Connie in a raspy voice. "There's a reason why my friendship with your parents went sour." Connie hunched over and cupped a wrinkled hand to the side of her mouth, ready to tell me something secretive. I looked into her bloodshot eyes.

"Eleanor wanted to borrow money from me. I asked what the loan was for, and she said they needed to build up their bank account for the child welfare investigation. We trusted Eleanor, so I lent her ten thousand dollars, our entire life savings. It was just a temporary thing. Eleanor promised to pay us back right after the adoption went through, but she never did. They kept the money and avoided us from then on.

"There never *was* a child welfare investigation. The next thing I knew, your parents moved away and we never saw them or the money again. John and I knew they must have been in terrible trouble, so we just let it go."

"I'm sorry, Connie," I said. "I had no idea."

Connie reached out and grabbed my hands. Her translucent skin was soft and cold to the touch.

"It's not your fault, dear. They did it for you. Your

parents loved you very much. Eleanor and Artie were good people and I've forgiven them, but they borrowed all that money and went through something awful and never shared it with anyone. I wish they hadn't brought me into it."

The story was devastating. Bad things happened to my parents, and it was lost to the past.

"Is there anything else you can tell me?" I asked.

Connie thought for a moment. "Well, I don't want to hurt your feelings any more than I already have, but we weren't the only ones who loaned money to Eleanor. She borrowed another ten thousand dollars from people in Artie's family, but never told him. That money wasn't re-paid either, and it destroyed Eleanor's relationship with them."

It was a kick in the gut, and I rose from the chair. Twenty thousand dollars disappeared, and The Sisters resented Eleanor for the loss.

Saltzman's secretary put me right through to him. "Who was the real contact person between Doris and Eleanor?" I demanded.

"Connie Taylor," answered Saltzman.

"That's not true. I went to see Connie Taylor, and she denied having any involvement with my adoption."

"Pat, your parents provided all the information in the adoption report. I confirmed that Connie Taylor and Doris Sochek worked at the Newark Public Library."

"Connie insisted she never met Doris."

"As far as I knew it was Mrs. Taylor. What *difference* does it make?"

"It makes a lot of difference! Eleanor borrowed ten thousand dollars from the Taylors, and another ten thousand from the Callahans. Where did that money go, Mr. Saltzman?"

"I don't like what you're insinuating."

"I'm just asking a question. You were my parents' attorney and you're supposed to protect their interests. A lot of money changed hands."

"It sounds like a shakedown," he remarked. "Your parents must have paid someone to conceal information they wished to keep quiet. I was not involved in that aspect.

"I received a modest legal fee and reimbursements for a few small expenses. That's all. I would never take a large cash payment from Eleanor, or anyone else for that matter."

"Then the money went to my birth mother."

"I doubt it. She was impoverished. Look, you're asking me about things that happened forty years ago. Most of the people involved are gone now, including your birth mother. That money is long gone, too. You should forget about the past and take care of your family. Your birth mother was a troubled woman and you're better off without her."

"I appreciate your advice and concern, Mr. Saltzman, but I have to know everything."

His tone went cold. "Take care, my boy."

Finding Doris wasn't going to be easy. No phone book in the tri-state area listed her name. Municipal employees tried to help me, but their efforts failed. The Internet was in its infancy, and I wasn't proficient with a computer. I only knew that Doris Sochek was born in Mountainside, New Jersey on August 1st, 1929, so I ordered a copy of her birth certificate.

Doris Waldheim was her maiden name. Father George worked as a chauffeur and mother Helen was a homemaker. The information was interesting, but offered no help.

It was New Year's Eve 1996. Judy Forman stopped by the house with a copy of the *Essex County White Pages*. "You should look for William Van Winkle," she said. "If he still lives in the area, you might be able to find Doris through him."

Flipping through the phone book, I found only one person listed by that last name, *Van Winkle, William - 10 Valley Road, Redmond*. He never left town. I circled the street in red on a Redmond map and it intersected another circle I'd drawn around Hillside Avenue. William lived close to my parents' old home. Without giving myself a chance to think, I dialed the phone number and someone picked up on the first ring.

"Hello?" said the voice of an older man.

"Are you William Van Winkle?" I asked.

"Yes."

"Were you born on July 8th, 1928, and did you join the army during the Second World War, then take a job as a shipping clerk with Acme Lines?"

There was silence. "How do you know all those things about me?"

"Because I'm your son."

"What?" he gasped. "It can't be. Where did you come from?"

"I came from your relationship with Doris Sochek."

"Doris who?"

"Doris Sochek. You were seeing her in January of 1956, and she gave birth to me in October. It's all in my adoption record."

"I never heard of the woman."

"You're the right William Van Winkle, aren't you?"

"Someone gave you a lot of personal information about me without my consent. You said you're adopted?"

"Yes, by the Callahans. Did you know them?"

He didn't respond. "Listen, I have a lot of explaining to do. I'm sitting next to my wife and she heard everything."

"Why don't we meet?" I asked. "I can look at you, and you can look at me, and we'll see what we think."

"Maybe," he answered.

CHAPTER 7

Eddie Snow was a childhood friend from Bedford. He worked for the Essex County Prosecutor's Office, and still lived in the original Snow family home with his wife and children. Many years had passed since we last spoke, and with much hesitation, I called him on a Sunday afternoon to ask for his help.

"Eddie, a strange thing happened to me. I found out Eleanor and Artie adopted me at birth."

"We always told you that," said Eddie.

His statement blew away forty years of denial. The neighborhood kids told me from the beginning that I was adopted, but I refused to believe them. Their mothers and fathers whispered about it at family parties and school functions, and the kids heard the gossip. My parents continually denied the rumor, and convinced me that an only child was always accused of being adopted. That deception worked for four decades, until Aunt Elizabeth shattered the myth with her overdue confession.

Eddie and I spent an hour rehashing my life story, from the day we met on the street at age five to Eleanor's funeral.

"There were whispers at O'Reilly's Funeral Home in 1978," said Eddie. "People wondered if you knew."

"I didn't know," I insisted. "Eleanor's death put me into hibernation."

"That's when we lost touch. It's my fault for not calling you all those years."

"Don't blame yourself, Eddie. Friendship is a two-way street."

It was a positive reunion. Eddie regretted not explaining the facts of life to me in full, and I should've listened to my friends back then. The immaturity of youth and blind faith in Eleanor and Artie prevented me from seeking the actual truth.

I told him the story of my adoption discovery and replayed the conversations with William Van Winkle and

Connie Taylor. He promised to help me solve the puzzle that Eleanor and Artie left behind.

"I'll run Doris Sochek's name through the motor vehicle database. If she has a New Jersey driver's license, the name will pop up."

It was 11 p.m. on Thursday night, February 1st, 1997. I dozed off on the couch while Tina watched TV. The sound of a ringing telephone startled me and I grabbed the receiver.

"I found her," said a voice.

"What?"

"I found your birth mother."

"Eddie? Where is she?"

"Doris Sochek lives at 13 Summit Avenue in Redmond. She was arrested twice for DWI and leaving the scene of an accident. She's on the revoked list."

"My God, what's going on?"

"*Both* of your birth parents live in Redmond."

Eddie hung up and I was wide-awake. Tina waited for the update. "She's in Redmond," I said.

"It's a small town," said Tina. "Why didn't Howard Saltzman know that?"

I jumped off the couch and ran to the Essex County map spread out on the dining room table. Tracing the third red ring around Summit Avenue in an inverted Ballantine Ale insignia, I came to the stunning realization that all three addresses were within one block of each other.

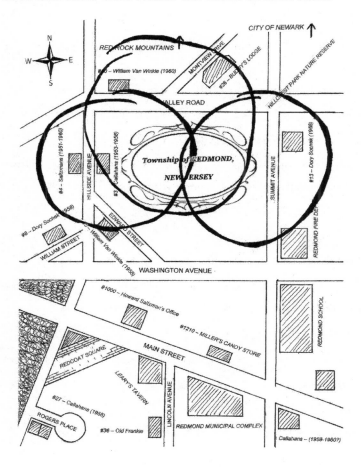

I faced Tina with a look of horror. "Doris lives one block from William Van Winkle, and one block from my old home. Saltzman's been lying all along."

The red Saturn station wagon climbed the hilly streets of Redmond, and Tina studied the map while Clare sang to herself. It was a trip back in time to a place I left long ago.

The landscape in Redmond hadn't changed at all since the 1950's. Cobblestone streets and neatly lined Belgian block curbs surrounded a town full of stores, Victorian mansions, and post-war Cape Cods. A variety of small apartment buildings dotted Redmond's landscape, some quaint and others dilapidated. It was a melting pot of the poor working class living down the hill and the rich white-collar professionals living up the hill.

3 Hillside Avenue was an ordinary-looking Cape Cod. Tina handed me a small black-and-white realtor's photograph of the house from 1953. It was the only record of our time spent there. I held up the snapshot for comparison and the house looked the same, except for new vinyl siding that covered the cedar shingles. The photograph brought to mind a story Artie once told me.

"3 Hillside Avenue was an ordinary-looking Cape Cod."

Before my birth, Artie surprised Eleanor with a brand new powder blue Pontiac for their anniversary. A thrilled Eleanor begged Artie to paint the exterior of the house the same color as the car. Artie purchased several cans of paint tinted to match the blue Pontiac, and spent several weekends brushing it onto the house. He smiled as Eleanor giggled and applauded him on the front lawn upon completion. Now bland vinyl siding covered the blue shingles.

"What a nice little house," remarked Tina.

I pointed to an identical Cape Cod across the street. "Number four. That's where Howard Saltzman lived. He sold it right after his divorce from Elsie."

We drove up the block and turned right onto Valley Road. A ramshackle, gray colonial sat on the left-hand side, surrounded by a collapsed wraparound porch and rotted steps. An unstable roof leaned over the entrance with a crude number ten nailed to the wall. Tina studied the map and motioned to the house.

"That's William Van Winkle's place," she said.

"I can't believe my real father lives in a house like that," I pined.

"Artie was your real father, Patrick. None of these people were there for you. You have to remember that."

I acknowledged her statement and rolled the car past Van Winkle's house. "Let's meet Doris first, then we'll pay William a visit."

Summit Avenue ran parallel to Hillside Avenue, and Doris' apartment building looked out of place in the modest residential neighborhood. It was a crumbling 1950's-era building constructed of tan brick with black rusted lanterns at the entryway. Rock-throwing vandals shattered the glass long ago. A dry brown Christmas wreath hung on the weathered wooden door and swung in the bitter wind. It exposed a blackened number 13. Several scruffy teens appeared out of the shadows, laughing and jabbing each other as they strutted down the street.

"I'll go to the door myself," I said. "You lock the car and leave it running."

The teenage gang passed by, and I sprinted off to the sound of automatic locks clicking behind me. A crusty doorknob grated as I entered the foyer, and crisp leaves and dry newspapers crunched beneath my feet. The place smelled rotten.

Five black mailboxes lined the wall. To the right was a row of door buttons numbered one through five, topped by a battered intercom. The crude name card for mailbox number one caught my attention: *Sochek/Waldheim/Barry*. The names *Sochek* and *Waldheim* were correct, but I was unsure of *Barry*. It offered hope that Doris remarried after my birth. An offensive buzzer reverberated throughout the first floor unit, but no one answered after three tries.

I pushed through the foyer door and walked back into the cold. By now it was pitch dark, and gangs of hoodlums wandered the neighborhood close to my car. I had to get back to Tina and Clare.

A glimmer of light shone through Doris' sheer window curtain. I pressed my face against the glass with both hands cupped around my eyes. There was a lit floor lamp in the living room, accented by the flicker of a television and the sound of canned laughter. Someone was home.

An easy chair and aluminum tray table sat across from the television, with a plate of steaming food on it and a half-drank glass of beer. A cigarette burned in the ashtray. Tufts of blonde hair jutted out from behind the chair, and I rapped hard on the window. The woman remained hidden.

Flashing car headlights caught my eye. Tina was signaling me to chase a gang of juveniles gathered around our car. I ran toward them yelling like an Apache warrior, and the startled thugs disappeared into the night. The locks snapped open and I jumped into the car.

"What happened?" asked Tina.

"Doris is home, but she's hiding," I answered. "She knows it's me."

"How could Doris know that?"

"I don't know. Somebody tipped her off." Tires

skidded as I pulled away from the curb and sped down Summit Avenue. "The lights and television are on in her apartment and somebody with blonde hair is hiding behind the chair."

"Let's find a diner where we can figure this out," said Tina.

We entered the downtown district and found ourselves on Main Street. At the corner of Lincoln Avenue, I spotted a pub called Leary's Tavern. Eleanor and Artie mentioned this place many years ago. It was an historic tavern once visited by George Washington during the American Revolution.

Redmond was steeped in colonial history, right down to the town center known as Redcoat Square. Patriots gunned down British soldiers there during a Revolutionary battle that took place outside Leary's Tavern. I guess the Irish somehow had a hand in it.

It was an archaic place, dank and nicotine-ridden with old wooden floors that smelled of stale beer. Barflies howled at off-color jokes, while toothless men in greasy clothes and a wizened old lady with wild hair scrutinized us. They looked like characters straight out of the French Revolution.

"Can I help you?" asked the ruddy-faced bartender. He looked to be seventy years old, but I couldn't be sure. The man adjusted his black bowtie against a starched white shirt and wrinkled his bulbous nose at me.

"I'm looking for a woman named Doris Sochek," I replied.

The bartender raised a hand to his chin and pondered the question. "Doris Sochek. That doesn't sound familiar."

"My name is Patrick Callahan. I just came from Doris' apartment."

He offered a wet hand and said, "My name is Clyde; pleased to meet you. Where does Doris live?"

"Summit Avenue."

Clyde grinned and let out an asthmatic laugh. "Oh, Big Dory! She's a regular here."

Tina rolled her eyes and Clare laughed. For a minute, I lost my sense of humor and motioned for Clyde to meet me at the quiet end of the bar to talk. We huddled close and I said, "Tell me about Dory."

"She's a tall woman, about six-foot. She had a bunch of kids."

"Is she married?"

"Nah, Big Dory hasn't been married in forty years.

She had lots of crazy boyfriends, though. I threw her out a bunch of times for fighting. Dory gets drunk and violent, but she's a real nice person." He smiled. "Why are you looking for her?"

"I'm her son."

An old man whipped around on his bar stool and yelled, "You, too?" The bar crowd burst into hysterics, which prompted Clyde to yell, "Knock it off!" It was a deflating moment. The more I learned about Dory, the more disappointed I became.

"Dory's home, but she won't answer the door," I said. "Do you have a phone number for her?"

"No, but I know somebody who does." He whistled toward the far end of the bar. "Hey, PJ! Come here!"

On command, a tall thin drunk jumped from his bar stool and knocked it to the floor. Again the crowd roared. He stumbled toward us with a burning cigarette clenched in his decayed teeth. A flannel shirt hung over crumpled jeans that covered his work boots, and a baseball cap crowned a nest of curly blond hair.

"What's up?" yelled PJ.

"These folks want to see Big Dory," said Clyde.

PJ pulled the cigarette from his mouth. "Why don't

they just call her?" His lungs crackled with demented laughter.

"They don't have Dory's phone number, wise guy. Take them up to Old Frankie's place so he can call her. This is Dory's son."

PJ looked at me with watery eyes that swam in his head, and a crazy broad smile spread across his face. "Nice to meet you. Follow me."

The tavern door slammed behind us, and we climbed the Lincoln Avenue incline. PJ sped so far ahead I had to run to catch up, and Tina grabbed my arm to keep pace.

"Who is Old Frankie?" I asked.

"He's a friend of your mother," replied PJ, as he veered in a serpentine pattern. Tina gave a nervous giggle as PJ stopped short at 36 Lincoln Avenue. He climbed the wooden steps to the covered porch, banged on the door, and walked inside. Tina huddled close with Clare between us. I kissed her on the forehead and waited.

With a bang, the front door flew open and some unseen force catapulted PJ onto the porch like a cannon ball. He stumbled down the steps with a lit cigarette in his mouth and a crazed young woman behind him.

"Lighting a cigarette in the house while my grandfather's on oxygen!" she shouted. "*Is he crazy? He'll blow us all to kingdom come!*" She looked at me. "Are you Dory's son?" I nodded and a smile replaced the scowl on her face. "I've known her since I was a little girl."

We stepped inside the dingy house and walked down a narrow hallway. The young woman stopped in front of an old man sitting on the living room couch. He looked like Artie, and it startled me.

"Grandpa," said the young woman. "This is Patrick Callahan. He's Dory's son."

The old man offered a skeletal hand and said, "I'm Frankie." A ragged blanket covered his small frame, and he struggled to breathe through an oxygen tube. Hair once dark was thin and white; eyes once full of life were sad and hollow. It was like standing in Artie's living room again, wondering how much time he had left.

"He has emphysema," said the young woman. "Grandpa used to smoke."

"I understand," I said. "I'm Doris Sochek's long-lost son. She gave me up for adoption at birth."

"Oh," said Frankie. "Let me call her for you." He struggled to dial the number and put the portable phone to his ear. "Dory? Your son Patrick is here. He wants to talk to you." He stopped to listen and looked at me with droopy eyes. "She's afraid."

"Tell her both of my parents are gone and I never knew about her."

Frankie repeated the phrase and put the phone in my hand. I said, "Hello?"

"Patrick? Is it really you?" said a woman's voice.

"Yes. I just found out that I'm adopted and I've been searching for you."

Dory sighed. "I never wanted to give you up, but I had to. My husband left me alone and I couldn't afford another baby. Who's with you?"

"My wife Tina and daughter Clare."

"I'm so glad you're married with a child." She hesitated. "Are you *sure* your parents never talked about me?"

"No, they never said a word."

"Can you come back to my apartment? I didn't know who was ringing my bell before. I thought it was a Jehovah's Witness or something. Please come back."

"Of course. Can I bring you anything?"

"A six-pack of Budweiser. Use the back entrance to my place."

We hurried out of the house and into the inviting night air.

"Dory wants beer," I said.

"Then I'll take a bottle of wine," responded Tina.

PJ leaned against the front porch post snoring, and awoke to the slam of a storm door. He took us on a drunken walk back to Leary's, and I gave him five bucks for his trouble.

Clyde met me at the bar with a grin. "Frankie looks like the guy on the poison bottle, don't he?" I didn't reply as he opened the cooler and slid a six-pack of Budweiser long necks into a brown paper bag. "Dory likes Bud in bottles."

"I need white wine, too," I said.

He burst out laughing and turned on me like an ungrateful waiter. He faced the group of patrons huddled at the bar and yelled, "Hey, folks! He wants to know if we have *wine!*" An onslaught of laughter battered my ears. Even PJ joined in, and I felt like taking my five bucks back.

"Never mind," I said. A round of applause followed as we dashed out the door to search for a liquor store.

We arrived at Dory's building, and I found the back entrance near a detached two-car garage. I knocked and a woman's sweet voice said, "Come in."

A tall, gangly woman with bleached-blonde hair leaned against the kitchen sink smiling. "Eleanor never told you about me?" she asked. I shook my head and the woman extended her arms. "I'm Dory. Patrick Joseph... it's been so long."

She breezed across the room and hugged me, whispering, "I've missed you." My briefcase and package goods fell to the countertop in a surreal embrace. Dory moved back and held my hands to look at me, then leaned forward for a kiss, but I turned away. She smelled of cigarettes and alcohol, and something about her face bothered me. Undeterred, Dory focused on Tina and Clare. "You must be Patrick's wife."

"I'm Tina, and this is Clare."

"Oh, what a lovely name." With that, Dory whisked Clare from Tina's arms, and I assured my worried wife that it was all right. Dory clung tightly onto Clare and flashed me a regretful face. "I had to let you go, Patrick. There was no money, and I wanted a better life for you."

"What about your other children?" I asked.

Dory pouted. "They're all gone." She handed Clare back to Tina and grinned. "Why don't we sit in the dining room?" I grabbed two bottles of beer and joined them.

We sat at a worn pine table. Dory snatched a Budweiser from my hand, twisted the cap off, and offered a toast. "To a happy reunion," she said, and guzzled down half the bottle.

"Who is my real father?" I asked.

Dory looked me in the eyes and said, "Karl Sochek."

"I know it's not Karl Sochek. The adoption report states that William Van Winkle is my birth father."

A guilty expression cloaked Dory's face. "Yes, he's the one." She lit a cigarette and inhaled. "Oh, Billy, we were so close in those days. I dated him for a while and it was a beautiful experience."

"Now you live one block from each other."

Dory took a deep swallow of beer. "Billy moved into the neighborhood years ago, but it was just a coincidence. I never told him about you."

"Billy knows about me now. I called him a month ago, and he said he's never heard of you."

"He said that? Why, I see him on the street every day walking his little dog. I'm gonna talk to him about this!" She grew agitated and chugged down the rest of the beer.

"Let's call him right now," I said.

"No!" replied Dory. "I don't want to upset his wife.

I'll try Billy tomorrow afternoon when she's at work, to straighten things out." She jumped up and traipsed to the kitchen, returning moments later with a single beer bottle.

"Tell me about Karl Sochek," I said.

"Good old Checky," remarked Dory, as she dropped into the chair. "He was a union carpenter and a heavy drinker. Spent most of his time in taverns and left me alone with the kids."

"I heard he left you because Billy was my father."

"Checky was just irresponsible," slurred Dory."He was a no good drunk who died in a bar fight." Tina looked at me in disbelief. There was a crazy, dreamy look in Dory's eyes.

"Billy married my best friend, Candy, but he didn't love her. He loved me because I made him happy. Checky got loaded one night and stumbled out of the house, and the cops found him dead the next morning with a gash in his head." Dory slapped the empty beer bottle against her hand and swayed in the chair. She peeled the label off and muttered something.

"Who is Lana?" I asked. "She called Howard Saltzman on November 25th, the day after I found out I was adopted."

Dory's face lit up. "That's my sister, Lana McGovern. She lives in Toms River."

My heart raced. "That's just fifteen minutes from me. A woman named Connie Taylor lives in Toms River, too, and she worked with you at the Newark Public Library. That's how you met Eleanor."

"I *never* worked at the library, and I don't know anybody named Connie Taylor. The nurse in my obstetrician's office told Eleanor about me. Her name was Elsie."

"Elsie Saltzman?"

"Yes. She sent Eleanor to my apartment pretending to be a social worker, but I saw right through it. Eleanor cried and begged me to go through with the adoption." The empty beer bottle crashed to the table and Dory was officially drunk. She leaned closer. "You know, I never met Artie. I think she worked this whole deal on her own. Are you sure they didn't tell you about me?"

Her statement offended me. "My parents never mentioned your name, but Artie was still proud to have me as his son. He named me Patrick Joseph after his father."

Dory exploded. "*I* named you Patrick Joseph!" She charged into the bedroom as Tina clung onto me.

"Patrick, we have to get out of here. I'm afraid for Clare."

"I know. We'll leave soon. Thank God Eleanor came

for me."

Dory returned in a docile manner with a large black scrapbook tucked under her arm. Howard Saltzman was correct; she was psychotic.

"Nobody's ever seen this photo album," said Dory. "It's filled with pictures of you and me, Patrick."

Dory laid the photo album on the table and lingered over me as cigarette smoke wafted around my head. She encouraged me to open the heavy cardboard cover. The album contained an organized series of photographs that detailed my birth and five-day stay in the hospital. An exact written narrative accompanied each picture with frightening accuracy.

Flipping to the last page, I was struck by the image of a dark, silhouetted woman standing outside the hospital. She was dressed in a kerchief, dark sunglasses, and tweed coat. The lady resembled the stranger in my flashbacks.

"Who is that?" I asked.

"Oh, that's me," answered Dory.

A flood of horrible memories rushed forth as I sat in shock and stared at the page, but none of it made sense to me. Dory leaned over and pulled two photographs from the album. She handed them to me with the words,

"These are for you."

My hands trembled as I took the ancient Polaroids. The picture in my left hand depicted a solemn-faced Dory, posed on a hospital bed holding a newborn baby boy. The photo in my right hand showed a young Eleanor Callahan sitting in a black Studebaker, dressed in a coat and white kerchief. She held a smiling baby swathed in linen.

I slipped the photographs into my coat pocket and hustled Tina and Clare out of the apartment. Dory whirled around in shock.

"Patrick," she cried. "When will you come back?"

Sochek/Waldheim/Barry beckoned me from the mailbox in the cold foyer.

"I forgot to ask her about the name *Barry,*" I said.

"It's probably another dead husband," quipped Tina.

"The photo in my right hand showed a young Eleanor Callahan sitting in a black Studebaker, dressed in a coat and white kerchief. She held a smiling baby swathed in linen."

CHAPTER 8

On Monday afternoon, I burst into Howard Saltzman's office. An older woman sat at the front desk and studied me through thick glasses.

"Can I help you?" she asked.

"I demand to see Mr. Saltzman. He arranged my adoption and I have questions for him."

"Mr. Saltzman is having lunch and doesn't wish to be disturbed, especially by someone who just barged into this office without an appointment."

My aggressive approach didn't work, and I regretted the outburst. In a soft tone I said, "I'm trying to come to terms with my adoption. I need more information."

"I'm sure Mr. Saltzman told you everything he knows."

I shook my head. "The trouble is, he *hasn't* told me everything."

The secretary tapped her fingernails on the desk and thought for a moment, then looked at me with an air of maternal understanding. Picking up a pen, she scrawled something onto a yellow legal pad, tore it off, and held it up. "Just remember, I didn't give this to you." The note read, *Buddy's Lodge, 26 Montview Drive.* "It's a popular tavern up the mountain near the Hillcrest Park Nature Reserve. You can't miss it."

Buddy's Lodge resembled a ski chalet set in the Red Rock Mountains. The summit's red clay beauty and snow-capped peaks rose high above the structure. Eleanor and Artie dined at this establishment during their young and carefree days.

Countless photographs of famous figures covered the walls. Actors and actresses from a bygone era, sports figures, presidents and notorious mob figures, flanked by studio portraits of veteran politicians from Essex County. Buddy's Lodge was quite a place in its heyday.

"How many?" asked the hostess.

"Actually, I'm here to see someone," I replied.

"Howard Saltzman. Do you know him?"

The hostess smiled. "Table twenty-four." We navigated past several packed tables with people talking and eating, as waitresses flew by us in an orchestrated ballet of table service. "There he is," she said, pointing toward a private booth.

Howard Saltzman wore a gray suit with a napkin tucked under his chin. He lurched forward to slurp his soup, and looked up at me as I approached and sat across from him.

"Patrick," he said. "What brings you here?"

"I have to talk to you," I replied.

Saltzman wiped his mouth with the napkin and asked, "Oh, what about?"

"I found my birth mother, Dory Sochek."

"Yes, I know. She phoned me this morning to thank me." Saltzman went back to spooning soup into his mouth and I sat in disbelief.

"What else did she say?"

"Nothing. She's just grateful you came back to her. That's all."

"You knew that Dory and Billy Van Winkle still lived in Redmond. Instead of telling me the truth, you said *the trail is cold.*"

A waitress buzzed to the table and dropped a plate of food in front of Saltzman. He picked up a tuna sandwich on rye toast and took a huge bite. With a mouth full he said, "It wasn't my place to tell you where she lived. You needed to find her on your own."

I glared at him. "Dory never worked at the Newark Public Library, and Connie Taylor had no involvement with my adoption. It was Elsie who accompanied Eleanor to the hospital to pick me up."

Saltzman took a gulp of coffee. "That's true. I'd forgotten Elsie went with Eleanor. That detail slipped my mind."

"Elsie worked as a nurse for Dory's obstetrician. Did that slip your mind, too?"

"I don't appreciate the sarcasm."

"Then stop lying, Mr. Saltzman. You knew Connie Taylor wasn't the go-between."

The discussion exploded into a full-blown argument. We battled over my adoption, trading facts and throwing barbs until a frustrated Saltzman slammed his fists onto the table. The empty cup and spoon flew into the air and crashed to the floor. The hostess dashed across the silent dining room and stopped at the table.

"Mr. Saltzman!" she commanded. "If this fighting continues, you'll have to leave. You're upsetting the other patrons." She slapped the guest check onto the table.

Saltzman smiled and patted her hand. "I apologize, Gladys. It's over now."

The lunch crowd returned to their meals, and the sound of a thousand conversations continued. Howard Saltzman looked at me like a concerned uncle.

"Patrick, I'm starting to worry about you. Leave the past alone and stay away from the people you're asking me about. They're a bad bunch."

"How do you know that?"

His expression went cold. "I just know." Saltzman slid the guest check across the table and stood. "There's nothing more to say."

He walked out of the restaurant and left me with the food bill.

I left Buddy's Lodge and drove to Dory's apartment unannounced. She was lounging on the living room couch smoking a cigarette and drinking a bottle of beer. It was twelve-thirty in the afternoon. Dory appeared agitated and didn't say hello.

"What's wrong?" I asked.

"I had a big fight with Billy this morning, and his wife grabbed the phone and told me to leave them alone." Dory sighed. "Billy walks his dog at exactly three o'clock every day. I'll stop him tomorrow and patch things up."

"You called Howard Saltzman."

"Yes, to thank him for bringing my son back to me."

"Are you sure that's the only reason?" Dory said nothing. "Tell me all about your relationship with Eleanor."

Dory smiled. "Oh, she was a sweet woman, but the poor thing was addicted to drugs. Eleanor visited me twice a week during my pregnancy and I thought we were friends. Then she took you away from me and ignored my phone calls. That upset me. I felt so used."

"So you admit to calling her," I said.

"Once or twice," replied Dory.

I moved toward the door and Dory sprang from the couch crying. "Don't you love me, Patrick?"

I looked into her eyes and replied, "I'm just getting to know you. Love comes later."

Leary's Tavern was quiet that afternoon. I wandered in

for no particular reason and sat at the bar. Clyde recognized me right away.

"Zinfandel or Chardonnay?" he joked.

"Very funny," I replied. "A Bud draft, please."

The pint glass overflowed and saturated the bar top, but Clyde just smiled and wiped it up with a towel. "So, I heard you had a nice reunion with Big Dory."

"A reunion of sorts," I answered. "Look, Clyde, can you tell me the full story of Big Dory Sochek?"

He looked around the bar. There was one drunk falling asleep in his scotch glass and a table of old-timers reading *The Racing Form.*

"Five of her boyfriends died under dubious circumstances," said Clyde. "The cops found two dead in their cars from carbon monoxide poisoning, one hanged himself in Dory's garage, and two others died of stab wounds. Even Karl Sochek ended up dead on the street in Newark back in the fifties."

"Dory claimed it happened in a bar fight."

Clyde shook his head. "Karl died two blocks from home, and there wasn't a bar in the neighborhood. The cops found broken glass in his scalp, like somebody hit him over the head with a bottle. They had no proof that Dory did it, and she's been collecting Karl's Social Security benefits since. She fled Newark and moved here around 1956."

"Dory has three names on her mailbox, *Sochek/Waldheim/Barry*. Where does the name *Barry* fit in?"

"Gordon Barry," answered Clyde. "Another boyfriend. He had terminal cancer, and Dory talked him into signing his life insurance policy over to her before he died. Gordon's kids were pretty upset about that, and Dory said they just wanted his money." Clyde laughed. "Pretty *ironical*, don't you think?"

"Very," I replied.

"Dory's a grifter who teamed up with her sister Lana. They ran around with cops back then, even the married ones. That kept them out of jail."

The bar clock read quarter to three, and I remembered Dory saying that Billy Van Winkle walked his dog every day at 3 p.m. With a quick goodbye, I dashed out the door and climbed into my car. As if on cue, Dory came around the corner, and I prayed she didn't notice my red station wagon. I held my breath and crouched down in the front seat, but Dory looked straight ahead. She was on a clear mission to drink. The door of Leary's Tavern closed behind her, and I drove off to meet my birth father.

————— ‹◊› —————

Billy Van Winkle stepped out the front door of his home with a small white dog tugging at the leash. He stopped on the broken-down porch and surveyed the neighborhood like a frightened rabbit. He was a gaunt man with gray hair, sad blue eyes, weak chin, and a prominent hooknose disproportionate to the rest of his face. I saw no resemblance to him at all.

Billy and the dog trotted down the steps and turned right, in the opposite direction of Dory's apartment. They rounded the corner on Hillside Avenue and I sprinted toward them. Billy moved pretty fast for a man who was nearly seventy years old. The dog sniffed around a tree by my old house, and I crept up behind Billy.

"Mr. Van Winkle," I said.

He whipped around with a startled look. "Yes?"

"I'm Patrick Callahan. We need to talk."

Billy pulled on the dog's leash and hurried away. "Look, I don't know this Dory person you asked me about." I followed him.

"That's not true. You've known her for many years. In fact, she called you this morning and you got into an argument. Isn't that right, Mr. Van Winkle?"

Billy kept walking with the yelping dog dragging behind. "I don't know anything!"

"Can you stop, please? I only want to talk to you. The secret's out, so you might as well tell me what happened."

Billy Van Winkle stopped and groaned. "My wife threatened to divorce me because of that woman. Tell her to leave me alone."

"Only if you give me the whole story."

He bent over and picked up the whimpering dog. "It all started back in early 1956, when we hung out with a gang that walked around in an alcoholic haze. I got involved with Dory and her best friend Candy. I married Candy not knowing Dory was pregnant with my child, and broke away from that group of drunks.

"Dory threatened to tell my wife about the pregnancy unless I paid her off in weekly beer money, and I agreed. Then she demanded more. I fell on hard times and couldn't pay her, so she told Candy about the baby." Billy looked away. "She divorced me."

"What happened after that?" I asked.

"I married Greta, a German immigrant from my church. Everything was good; I stopped drinking, landed a shipping clerk job, and bought a house on Valley Road in 1960. Fate landed me right down the block from Dory Sochek. She started shaking me down again, and threatened to tell Greta about my illegitimate son."

Billy cursed under his breath. "For thirty-five years I made payments, when I should've told Dory to go to hell! Greta's a religious woman and the truth is destroying her."

We stood facing each other with a quiet understanding of our mutual hardships. I looked into Billy's pathetic eyes. "If Greta is truly religious, she'll forgive you for the sins of the past."

Billy studied me with a series of contorted facial expressions. "I don't think it's true. There's no similarity between us." He vocalized exactly what I was thinking. Then a faint smile replaced the tightness in Billy's lips.

"If you *were* my son, I'd be proud of you."

DECADES *of* DECEPTION

CHAPTER 9

The heavyset librarian at the Newark Public Library waited for an answer.

"Nineteen fifty-three to nineteen sixty," I replied.

"I'll be right back."

She returned with eight metal canisters and pointed to a row of viewing monitors on the table. "Load each microfilm into the viewer and scroll down. Copies are five cents each." The librarian sat at the counter and read the latest edition of *The Essex County News.*

With red pen in hand, I spread my map on the table and analyzed eight years of *New Jersey Bell Telephone White Page Directories.* The microfilm records confirmed that AJ Callahan moved to 27 Rogers Place, Redmond in 1958. Now I had a physical address to go with the memory of that home. There was no listing for us in 1959. I circled each address on the map.

1953 to 1958: AJ Callahan - 3 Hillside Avenue, Redmond.

1953: Doris Sochek - 15 Trafalgar Drive, Newark. The Projects.

1953: William Van Winkle - 8 Newell Street, Newark.

1956: Doris Sochek - 8 William Street, Redmond.

1956: William Van Winkle - 5 Edward Street, Redmond.

1958: Doris Sochek - 13 Summit Avenue, Redmond.

1958: AJ Callahan - 27 Rogers Place, Redmond.

1959 to 1960: No listing for AJ Callahan.

1960: William Van Winkle - 10 Valley Road, Redmond.

Six intersecting circles surrounded the small neighborhood in Redmond. It proved that Dory and Billy stalked my parents, moving closer each time. Connie Taylor confirmed that twenty thousand dollars changed hands, and Howard Saltzman alluded to a shakedown. The evidence pointed to Dory and Billy. Rage built inside of me as I handed the librarian a five-dollar bill for copies.

I'd take the evidence to Billy Van Winkle right now and demand a confession before confronting Dory.

"I'll be right back with your change," said the librarian. My eyes focused on the obituary page of her newspaper. With morbid curiosity, I read one name in particular and let out a gasp.

WILLIAM VAN WINKLE 68

The librarian returned with my change and watched as I drew a red line through William Van Winkle's name on the printout.

"I'm so sorry," she said.

On a cold and windy Monday morning in late February 1997, I traveled a congested Route 280 north toward Redmond for a meeting.

I'd written a letter to Chief Michael Costello of the Redmond Police Department and chronicled the story of my adoption, the extortion, and possible kidnapping. The letter generated enough interest for a meeting at headquarters. The chief urged me not to speak with Dory until after we met, which prompted a barrage of phone calls from my birth mother begging for a visit. It took strong will not to tell her about the microfilm evidence I uncovered.

Billy Van Winkle was dead. Based on the violent visions that haunted me, the pair harmed me in a botched kidnapping attempt and the police rescued me. There had to be an incident report on file, and this was the perfect opportunity to ask for it.

The Redmond Police Department was housed in an old stone structure along with the court and records bureau. A police radio echoed behind the green-tinted bulletproof glass window as I approached, and it was dark except for the shadows of police officers milling about on the other side. A dispatcher's face appeared through a circular hole in the glass.

"Can I help you?"

"Yes, my name is Patrick Callahan. I have an appointment with Chief Costello."

The dispatcher nodded. "Sergeant Wilson will be right down to see you. Have a seat."

I was too nervous to sit and preferred to wander around the reception area reading the wanted posters. It wouldn't surprise me if Dory's face was on one of them. Ten minutes passed before a door swung open and a bearlike police officer appeared. He had red cropped hair and wore a friendly face.

"Patrick Callahan? I'm Gerry Wilson. I hear you've got quite a story to tell. I'm a third generation Redmond police officer, born and raised in town. My father and I know everything there is about Redmond and its people."

"Nice to meet you, sergeant," I said.

We reached the second floor detective bureau, abuzz with the sounds of ringing phones and clanging typewriters. Men in suits brushed past us and said good morning.

"It's chaos in here," said Sergeant Wilson. "Let's go see the chief."

The sign on the door read, "Chief Michael Costello." The sergeant knocked and a voice said, "Enter."

Chief Costello was a well-built man dressed in a blue pinstripe shirt and dark slacks. Sergeant Wilson introduced me, and the chief stood and offered his hand.

"Pleased to meet you, Mr. Callahan. Have a seat."

Sergeant Wilson sat next to me and studied my face, while Chief Costello pulled a large file from the drawer and read the cover.

"Doris Waldheim Sochek is your birth mother?"

"Yes, sir," I replied. "She put me up for adoption in 1956. Howard Saltzman made the arrangements and drew up the adoption papers."

He opened the police file and thumbed through decades of incident reports. Chief Costello explained that Doris Sochek instigated several drunken bar fights and perpetuated many confidence schemes on unsuspecting persons. She was an extortionist with a violent temper and psychotic tendencies, and left behind five dead boyfriends and one dead husband. The locals called her "The Black Widow of Redmond." According to the chief, Dory maintained her innocence on all counts.

"In 1956, someone struck Karl "Checky" Sochek on the head with a bottle," explained Chief Costello. "We believe it happened at home, and he died that night on a Newark sidewalk. There wasn't enough evidence to accuse Dory of the crime, and she moved to Redmond shortly thereafter."

"Say," added Sergeant Wilson. "Wasn't Dory Sochek arrested for prostitution several years ago?" The chief shot him an angry look. "I mean, that's what I heard."

"Dory was a *prostitute?*" I asked.

The Chief continued to stare at Wilson before turning my way. He was clearly annoyed. "Yes. I was getting to that and hoped to bring it up in a more delicate manner.

"During the 1950's, Dory Sochek and her sister Lana

McGovern worked in a brothel that operated above Miller's Candy Store at 1210 Main Street."

"That means she worked there at the time of my birth."

"I'm afraid so."

The two men paused for a moment while the information sank in. I was born from the union of a prostitute and a stranger, and the thought of it sickened me. Dory resorted to selling her own body for money, coupled with a chilling combination of kidnapping, extortion, and homicidal actions. She was capable of anything.

"Is there something specific you're looking for, Mr. Callahan?" asked the chief.

I struggled to recuperate from the devastating news, and said the first thing that came to mind.

"Dory Sochek and Billy Van Winkle took residences near my parents and demanded money. I remember being scalded in a hot shower and falling down a flight of stairs. The police brought me home with burns over my entire body."

Three sentences summed up my findings, and Chief Costello was sympathetic. "If Dory and Billy harmed you and harassed your parents, there's an incident report in our archives. The FBI handles child abduction cases. Either way, I'll assign an officer on light duty to search the records for any such report involving your family. We'll confine our search between the years 1956 to 1960. Does that sound right?"

"Yes," I replied.

Chief Costello rose from his chair. "Then it's settled. Sergeant Wilson will handle the case from now on, so please direct all phone calls and correspondence to him. I recommend that you stay away from Doris Sochek until we conclude a full investigation."

The sergeant faced me with an outstretched hand and a determined look. "Patrick, I'll do everything within my power to find the truth."

I left the Redmond Police Department that day feeling terrible. My thoughts wandered as I drove the streets of Redmond in a random pattern, with horrible childhood memories streaming before my eyes. The deeper I dug into the past, the more vivid the visions became.

Without thinking, I stopped my car across the street from 3 Hillside Avenue. The Cape Cod loomed against a bleak February sky, as I recalled my last conversation with Billy Van Winkle. He lived in fear most of his life, knowing that Dory wasn't far behind seeking more money, but that didn't excuse his criminal actions. I wondered if Billy resolved the conflict with his wife before dying.

A black 1950's Cadillac pulled up to the house. It was worn, rusted, and battered. The brakes squealed as the car ground to a halt at the walkway, and thick black smoke emanated from the tail pipes. The grimy driver's side window cloaked the profile of a woman wearing a kerchief. Thick sunglasses hid the stranger's eyes.

I ducked out of my car and edged up on the mysterious woman. Halfway across Hillside Avenue, she spotted me and sped off with tires screeching. A hail of gravel and exhaust sprayed my body, and I covered my eyes for protection.

The black Cadillac disappeared.

CHAPTER 10

It was a warm Saturday on the first day of March, and the Bell Telephone printout was in my hand as I entered the rear gate of Dory's apartment building. If she worked as a prostitute, I wanted her to admit it was true.

Chief Costello warned me to stay away from Dory during the police investigation, but my curiosity was too strong. I had to know if she conceived me in that local brothel, and I wanted the name of my birth father. Tina worried that I was pushing this search too far, but I reassured her everything was all right. I only had to convince myself that was true.

"Dory's not home!" shouted a rough-voiced stranger, glaring at me from a second-floor window.

"Do you know where she is?"

"She's at Hillcrest Park feeding the birds. Dory goes there every Saturday."

"Is that across from Buddy's Lodge?"

"Yeah." She slammed the window shut and closed the blinds.

The Hillcrest Park Nature Reserve was an idyllic place. It was abundant with rich forests and carpeted green lawns that rivaled any golf course. Wildlife flourished there, and tame deer grazed in open fields. Birds and tree-dwelling animals chattered as I pulled into the gravel parking lot. A footpath led to an opening in the trees, and there was Dory, perched on a bench tossing bread crusts to the birds. She didn't expect to see me.

"Patrick! How did you find me?"

"The old lady upstairs told me you were here."

Dory frowned. "Oh, her."

I sat on the bench. "I have bad news. Billy Van Winkle is dead."

She looked at me with a puzzled expression. "I wondered why all those people were at his house. Poor Billy, our last talk was an argument. I feel just awful."

Dory exhibited all the sincerity of a carnival huckster. She hummed to herself and splayed handfuls of crumbs to the pigeons and sparrows that gathered around her, calling each of them by name.

"Billy wasn't my father, was he?" I asked.

"Well, I wasn't sure," she replied. "There were so many men in my life back then I couldn't keep them straight. Now that I've studied your face, I know Jimmy is your father."

"Who's Jimmy?"

"James DeLaFrance. He was a Redmond cop I met at a bar in Newark right around the time I kept company with Billy. When I got pregnant with you, he dropped me like a bad habit, and I went to Billy for comfort. You look just like Jimmy."

DeLaFrance was such a phony name it made me laugh. Dory needed a scorecard to list the revolving door of lovers she entertained; no wonder she had problems identifying my father. That brought me to the primary reason for my visit, and I uttered the address, "1210 Main Street."

Dory's mouth fell open and her heavy eyelids widened, exposing green eyes set in a milky background. It was the first time I noticed her eye color.

"Miller's Candy Store," she whispered. Dory recovered fast, as always. Her sluggish eyes narrowed in a crocodilian stare that unnerved me. A smile replaced the oval curve of her mouth as she looked to the trees, and a hidden flock of birds responded with a cacophony of sound.

"I used to go there for penny candy when I was a little girl. Why do you ask?"

"I'm more interested in the time you spent there on the second floor," I replied. "At age twenty-six."

Dory gave me a dirty look. She knew exactly what I was talking about and her resentment was evident. "What do you mean?" she growled.

"The Redmond Police told me that you and Lana worked there as prostitutes. You sold yourself at the time of my birth."

She laughed. "Those cops will say anything to make me look bad. It's not true at all. Who are you going to believe: some donut-eating patrolman or your own mother?"

I remained silent and looked at her, signaling my obvious choice. Dory's face sank.

"Oh, Patrick, that's disappointing. How can you think such a thing of me?"

She burst into tears and her body seized. Dory dropped to the bench and transformed herself into the shape of a boa constrictor. She coiled around the bag of bread crusts like a hapless prey, and wailed like a baby. People stopped to look, and one man rushed over to help. I explained that a close friend died and I'd just broken the news to my "dear mother." The man understood and continued on his way.

"Dory!" I yelled. "Pull yourself together and stop this. You're play-acting and I'm not buying it."

The wailing stopped short, and Dory relaxed her contorted frame as she sat up. The tantrum ended with the flick of a switch and she turned her nose in the air. I had my answer; Dory was a prostitute in 1956, but she refused to talk about it. It was another example of reading into her behavior to uncover the correct answer.

Dory never made definitive statements; she only hinted at the truth in a flurry of false emotion and left the rest for me to figure out. I became an expert at interpreting Dory's psyche, and each revelation was more troubling than the last. I continued to question her.

"There's one more important question, and I want you to give me an honest answer. Did my parents pay you thousands of dollars?"

There was a sober look on Dory's face. "The Callahans gave me a little hush money, but not that much."

That admission fired my anger more than knowing my mother was a prostitute. I jumped up from the bench and grabbed both of Dory's arms. The flapping of wings and cries of escaping pigeons alarmed Dory, and she dropped the bag of bread crusts. The library printout fell from my coat pocket, and Dory watched as it floated to the bench.

"Why did my parents pay for your silence?" I screamed. "Tell me!" Dory tried to wrestle away from me, but I held on fast.

"I did what was necessary to survive!" she wailed. "Patrick, you're hurting my arms. Let me go!"

I grabbed the printout and crunched it in her face. "You stalked Eleanor and Artie. Phonebook records listed you and Billy within one block of my parents from 1956 to 1958. It was a shakedown!"

"It was just coincidental that Billy and me lived near your parents!"

"Why did they pay you?"

"Because I knew things." Dory stopped struggling and leered in my face. "Let go of me and I'll tell you." With strong hesitation, I released her arms and she gave me a stern look. "Now sit down." I grumbled and sat on the bench like an obedient child while Dory unraveled the printout and read the list of addresses. She knew I was close to cutting through her web of lies.

"That sleazy attorney Howard Saltzman took advantage of me. He doctored up some phony adoption papers and took you away. Eleanor knew it, and offered me money to keep you."

"How much?"

"I'm not sure. Maybe a thousand bucks."

"After you spent the thousand bucks, did you demand more?"

"No!" cried Dory. "I *never* asked for more money!" She wiped a manufactured tear from her eye. "Ask Howard Saltzman where the money went."

"You extorted cash from Billy Van Winkle, too. That's funny, since I wasn't his child. Then you scored your biggest windfall with Eleanor and Artie for many thousands. The Redmond Police believe you murdered five boyfriends and your husband, Karl Sochek."

Dory had a murderous look in her eyes. "Lies!" she bellowed. "I'm a victim. Everyone *used* me!"

"It's the other way around. You victimized every one of those men and you tortured my parents."

"How can you say that? I am your *mother!*"

"You were never a mother to me. You're a blackmailer and a murderer."

I stormed down the dusty park trail.

"You have reached Rocco Manetti – Private Investigator. Leave a message after the beep, and remember: don't panic!" That's what the voice on the answering machine said. I needed help to piece this complex story together, and one of my clients suggested that I contact this private eye. I left a long message and he called me back.

"Hey there, Mr. Callahan. You've got an interesting story and I can help you. Want me to stop over your house Saturday morning, say nine o'clock?"

"That would be fine," I answered.

I sipped my coffee and gazed out the kitchen window, waiting for Mr. Manetti's arrival. Tina washed the dishes while Clare wiggled in her bouncy seat and sang. We laughed at the originality of the impromptu song.

"Future songwriter," I observed.

"Like father, like daughter," said Tina.

The squeal of brakes brought me to the front door. Sunlight reflected off the windshield of a late model tan Mercedes Benz convertible parked outside. A barrel-chested man stepped out and slammed the door behind him. He took confident strides up the walkway and rang the doorbell.

"That's him," I said.

"He's a sharp dresser," remarked Tina.

She was right. Rocco Manetti was dressed in pressed tan slacks and a tan shirt, the same color as the Mercedes. His unbuttoned shirt revealed an outcrop of graying chest hair, covered in a tangle of gold chains. He pulled out a pocket comb and groomed his thick, black hair and cracked his neck as I opened the door.

"Mr. Callahan?" he asked.

"Yes," I replied. "Mr. Manetti?"

He smiled and extended his hand. "Hey, just call me Rocky." We shook and my knuckles cracked. I grimaced in pain.

"Nice to meet you, Rocky."

"You can always judge a man by his handshake."

He stepped inside and kissed Tina's hand, winking at her. "Hey, you're a beautiful lady, and look at *this* little baby doll!" He tickled Clare's chin. "Nice family you've got here, Mr. Callahan."

"Call me Pat," I said. "Why don't we go downstairs to the party room?"

"Sure," said Rocky. "Lead the way." We bounded down the steps to the finished basement and he took a seat at the bar.

"Can I get you coffee or water?" I asked.

Rocky thought for a second and said, "Scotch." It was just after nine o'clock in the morning.

I tossed a few ice cubes into a rock glass and poured a small amount of Dewar's Scotch. Rocky made a sign with his hand. "Three fingers," he instructed. I filled the glass half way and slid it across the bar. Rocky extended his pinky and took a sip, then wiped his mouth with the back of his hand.

"Good stuff," he remarked. "I usually drink wine, but when I saw the scotch bottle on the shelf, I had to have it." Rocky produced a notebook and pen. "Now, tell me everything from the beginning."

I launched into the story while he gave me his full attention, all the while scribbling in the notebook without looking down. I talked about Eleanor and Artie, Aunt Elizabeth, Dory and Lana, Howard Saltzman, and the late Billy Van Winkle.

"Well," declared Rocky. "We ain't getting any answers from *him*."

He speculated that Aunt Elizabeth Black was my real birth mother and not Dory, and Artie was my true father. I asked how he came to those conclusions, and the private eye went on a wild theoretical tangent that made no sense at all. I gave a look of disbelief. He thought for a second, pursed his lips, and remarked: "Okay, forget that scenario." Rocky dashed off a few more sentences and turned the notebook around. "Here are all the answers."

Long, squiggled sentences covered the paper in an indistinguishable prose, like a strange alien code. I couldn't decipher one word of it. Rocky smiled with all the confidence of a theatrical agent.

"What do you think? Pretty good, right?"

"I don't know. "

"Hey, all you have to do is give me a retainer of five hundred bucks and we'll get to the bottom of this whole thing. I'll interview your mother and that lawyer and they'll give me the answers." Rocky pointed to his head. "I know how to talk to these people. I use *psycho-logee*.

"You mean psychology."

"Yeah, that's what I said."

With serious doubts about this guy's abilities, I wrote a check for five hundred dollars. He snatched it off the bar and announced, "As soon as this clears, I'll get started." We shook hands to seal the agreement. This time, I bore down hard on Rocky's outstretched mitt and heard a crack. "You learn quick," he said with a grin. "Don't worry, this case is as good as solved."

Sergeant Wilson was on the phone. A group of retired Redmond cops demanded to know why the department had an interest in my alleged kidnapping. "Your story hints at a larger tale of corruption," remarked Wilson. "We didn't find anything yet, but the investigation generated some angry responses from those ex-cops."

"That's interesting," I said. "Dory claims a Redmond police officer named James DeLaFrance is my birth father."

"I heard that guy was crazy. He got in a jam years ago

and they fired him from the force."

James DeLaFrance was a real person, and a Redmond cop. That intrigued me.

"There's something else," I said. "Howard Saltzman forged my adoption records."

Wilson laughed. "Falsifying records is no stretch for that ambulance-chasing attorney. Sounds like you have the makings of a great book."

"I've kept a ledger since the beginning and I plan to write the story."

"I'll be the first to buy a copy."

A man named John Darling called me that night and said, "I hear you've been asking about Jim LaFrance."

"I'm searching for a James *DeLaFrance*."

"He's the same person. Jim shortened his name to LaFrance, just like the fire truck. He was my partner on the Redmond Police Force in the 1950's, and I have information if you're interested."

"Yes, I'm very interested. He's my alleged birth father."

There was no reaction to that statement, only a seamless continuation of our conversation.

"I think we should meet so I can tell you all about him.

How about the Pinnacle Diner in downtown Manasquan, say Friday at noon?"

The Pinnacle Diner was crowded at 11:45 in the morning. I sat in the first booth by the cashier's station and studied each person who passed by. The waitress handed me a menu.

"Is anybody joining you?"

"Yes. I'm expecting one other person."

Time passed and the clock on the wall read quarter after twelve. The waitress returned twice to take my order, and soon it was one o'clock. Odd that Darling was late, since he arranged the meeting. I surveyed the diner again, but no one looked the part of a seventy-year-old retired police officer.

A large man rose from the lunch counter and revealed a well-dressed gentleman with a flattop haircut seated next to him. The stranger shot me a look then turned away, as the waitress reappeared and blocked my view.

"Are you sure you wouldn't like something to drink?" she asked.

"Coke, please," I answered. She hurried off and the stranger with the flat top haircut was gone. *Damn it, I lost him*. I was about to race out of the diner when someone brushed against my arm. It was the stranger.

"Is your name John?" I asked.

"Yeah. John Smith."

He walked to the cashier's station and paid his check, then pushed his way through the crowded vestibule. I caught up with him on the sidewalk.

"Is your real name John Darling?"

The man looked at me with a forbidding stare and answered, "Yes."

"Why did you set up this meeting, then hide from me?"

"I wanted to see if you resembled Jim LaFrance. You do look like him."

"You've gone through a lot of trouble just for that. Did he put you up to this?"

"No, I did it out of my own curiosity, that's all. Again, I apologize for ignoring you." Darling walked away and I followed.

"Look, I need information about my birth father. Where does he live?"

Darling stopped. "Jim LaFrance died in 1980, one day shy of his fifty-third birthday. He was an alcoholic and drank himself to death after they fired him from the police

147

force."

It was a shot to the heart. I had four fathers, and not one of them was alive.

"Do you know a woman named Dory Sochek?" I asked. "She's my birth mother. Jim must have mentioned her name."

"Not to me," replied Darling, and he hurried away.

We sat at the dinner table and I twirled my string beans with a fork, thinking about Jim LaFrance and John Darling. Tina gazed out the window before turning my way.

"What's wrong?" she asked.

Before I could elaborate, the doorbell rang and Rocky Manetti peered through the glass. "Hey, there!" he called in a muffled voice. A shabby white Crown Victoria rumbled in the street and backfired like a shotgun as Rocky barged in. *"The Benz* is in the shop for an oil change and they lent me that clunker for the day. Say, I interviewed your mother this morning. She's a wonderful person!"

"Are you kidding?" I asked.

"You have to stop accusing her of all those terrible things. She's a beautiful lady and I have a dinner date with her Saturday night."

"You're crazy!" I shouted. "You're supposed to be working for me and you have a dinner date with a *suspect?*"

"That brings me to another point," said Rocky. "I stopped in to see Howard Saltzman. He's worried about you and I agree with him. You're starting to get paranoid."

That was it. I pushed Rocky out the door and locked it behind him. Tina had enough.

"Patrick, you've introduced all these crazy characters into our lives and they're not going to help you. Worst of all, Dory keeps calling the house and she's driving me crazy."

"What?" I said. "You never told me that."

"I didn't want to worry you. She calls me during the day and pretends to be interested in my home life with Clare. Dory keeps asking how we're getting along, digging for some weak point in our relationship. Something she can use against us, just like she did to your parents."

"It won't work. Dory doesn't have the same hold over us."

"Yes, she does - the truth! You want it so badly that she'll keep leading you on with false information to fire your interest. Dory's buying your affection, and it won't stop until you end the relationship."

"I have to get the full story."

"It won't come from her."

A mixture of confusion, anger, and frustration clouded my mind. I got up and circled the living room floor like a nervous boxer.

"Maybe you should seek professional help, Patrick."

"A psychologist?"

"If that gives you the answers you need, then *yes*."

CHAPTER 11

Dr. Albert Roseland was a clinical psychologist and one of my clients. He pushed his thick, gray hair aside and asked about my family. I said everything was fine except for the adoption discovery.

"That's what we're here to talk about," he said. "So tell me what happened."

I told him everything and concluded by saying I wanted to learn the absolute truth.

"I understand, Patrick. There are those who wish to know, and others who do not."

"It must be the Scorpio in me," I joked.

Dr. Roseland laughed. "Yes, Scorpios are inquisitive and passionate people.

"It's evident that the harsh treatment from your aunts is connected to your adoption. They've buried painful memories from the past, and you're a living reminder of those events. Instead of embracing you, they've chosen to turn away. Your aunts are misguided in their actions."

"I agree, but what can I do about it?"

"There's nothing you can do. You've tried every approach to reason with them to no avail. I'm afraid you can't change them, and you must come to terms with the past on your own.

"A preliminary diagnosis shows that you're suffering from depression, low self-esteem, and anxiety, all brought on by childhood trauma and the difficult relationship with your adoptive father. The discovery of your adoption brought all of this to the surface."

"It makes me wonder if Artie ever loved me as a son."

"I believe he did," said Dr. Roseland. "Artie had difficulty expressing that emotion toward you, torn between his loyalty to The Sisters and his dedication to Eleanor. They caught you in the middle.

"There's another side to this story that concerns me; your obsessive search is affecting your marriage, and Tina fears you're drifting away from her and Clare. I know it's difficult learning of your adoption at forty, and I understand your feelings of hurt and betrayal, but you can't let go of the present in search of the past."

The doctor was right, but my determination was too strong to back off now. I wrestled with my troubled conscience.

"Have you ever been under hypnosis?" asked Dr. Roseland. I said no, and he switched on a 1970's-vintage tape deck player. I heard the sounds of ocean waves breaking on the shoreline and the faint call of seabirds.

"This will relax you," he said. "Pull the handle on the right side of your chair and sit back. Do you mind if I tape record our session?" I didn't mind, and Dr. Roseland started the tape recorder.

"Now close your eyes and let all of the tension and stress fall away from you. I'll count the years backwards to 1958. That was the year in question, when traumatic things happened to you. Open your mind to the past."

My arms and legs became cement, and visions of a starlit night sky appeared before my closed eyes. The scene lightened while Dr. Roseland spoke in a monotone voice and recited the years in reverse. He stopped at certain years in particular.

"It's 1994."

I see Artie sitting at his kitchen table, smoking a cigarette and drinking coffee.

"The year is 1978."

Eleanor lies in a hospital bed with tubes attached to her.

"It's 1967."

I walk down the street in Bedford. It's summertime. Two ladies wearing sunglasses and kerchiefs smile down at me. One lady reaches out and takes my hand.

"It's December of 1966."

I'm in O'Reilly's Funeral Home. I can't hold Grandma Flora and we fall to the floor.

"It's 1960."

I step into a brand new house. My footsteps echo on the fresh hardwood floor as I hold hands with Grandma Flora and Grandpa Willy. Eleanor and Artie are there.

"Now it's 1959."

I'm sitting on a couch with Eleanor in an apartment. There's a small television with rabbit ears on the table.

"It's October of 1959."

The movie reel stops and becomes reality. It's my birthday, and I feel the strong rush of a cold autumn wind.

Swirls of red and gold leaves dance across the air, and I run around the yard trying to catch them. The small cap on my head is tight and so is the wool jacket I'm wearing.

A big black car stops along the hedges and a tall lady is standing over me. She smiles and looks familiar, like the ladies on the street in Bedford, but that's in the future. The lady wears dark sunglasses and a tweed coat and calls me "Patrick."

Eleanor rushes out of the house screaming. I see the number 27 on the big red front door. She grabs me and the lady jumps back into her car and peels away. Eleanor runs into the house screaming and grabs the telephone. Artie rushes in wearing a postal uniform.

Dr. Roseland's voice interrupted the experience. "It's October of 1958."

The date jolted me to another place in time. It's my birthday again, and I'm burning in a hot shower. Hands are holding me down. I escape and a woman's voice shouts, "I'm going to shove you!" before I tumble down a flight of wooden stairs, smacking my head on the floor. I awaken on the lap of a patrolman in a speeding police car. Cold ice cream drips from a cone onto my burned hand.

I bolted up from the armchair with my heart pounding.

Dr. Roseland clicked off the music and the tape recorder and said, "Take deep breaths and let them out slowly."

He played the tape. In a voice full of peaks and valleys, I narrated the trip through time. I cried out during the terrifying parts of the story and screamed at the end.

"You've taken a journey backward in time and witnessed repressed memories from the past in reverse order," explained Dr. Roseland. "This is called explicit flashback. Most children under the age of five experience implicit flashback with less detail, but your recollections are more adult in nature. Let me put the events into proper chronology so they make sense."

He read from a notepad. "On your second birthday in the fall of 1958, someone forced you into a hot shower for reasons unknown. That person pushed you down a flight of stairs, and you suffered neck and back injuries and gashes over each eye socket. The trauma forced you to block out the face of the stranger."

I rubbed my fingers along the deep scars hidden under my eyebrows. Eleanor told me they weren't scars at all, but natural creases. I accepted that explanation without question. A neurologist once diagnosed the subsequent blackout spells I suffered as a *short circuit in the brain.*

Dr. Roseland continued. "The event occurred in an undisclosed location. Do you remember your surroundings?"

"Yes. It was a dingy apartment."

"The next incident took place on your third birthday: October 29, 1959. The stranger always struck on that date. Eleanor left you alone on the lawn for just a minute and the lady tried to coax you into her car. Eleanor rescued you."

"That was 27 Rogers Place in Redmond."

"Yes, your family abandoned the house on Hillside Avenue and moved there."

"I remember now. It was an old Victorian duplex with high ceilings and stained glass windows in the dining room, like a church. I loved the red front door."

It explained why I always gravitated toward red fruits, candy, beverages, and vehicles. As a child, I ate the red paint off Christmas tree ornaments, and every picture I painted included the color red. 27 Rogers Place stayed with me throughout my life.

"Your parents fled to an apartment later that year," said Dr. Roseland.

"My parents insisted that we moved from Hillside Avenue to Bedford, but I knew there were two other places in between. I wasn't allowed outside the apartment. Eleanor and I spent the days there watching a small black and white television set, eating colored candy dots from strips of waxed paper. We laughed a lot and I spent countless hours drawing."

"Your family was hiding from the lady who approached you on the lawn," observed Dr. Roseland. "She was the person who put you in the hot shower."

"Was that Dory in disguise?" I asked. "How could she do those horrible things to me?

I walked into the house carrying a bouquet of flowers, and surprised Tina. She took them, hugged me, and began to cry. Tina was trying to understand what I was going through, but it was difficult.

"I'm afraid, Patrick. I don't want to live through the same nightmare as your parents. We don't know what happened to them, and dredging up the past is a bad idea."

"The hypnosis session uncovered a lot," I said. "I'm putting the pieces together and there's no turning back now."

It was pitch black when I walked to the back entrance of Dory's building and ran into the old woman from upstairs.

"Don't get too friendly with Dory," she warned. "She's devious and people end up dead. If Dory comes at you driving an old black Cadillac, run!" The woman pointed to the detached garage and vanished into the shadows.

The garage window was dirty, and it was too dark to see inside. I walked around front and found a heavy wooden door, and it squealed on the tracks as I struggled to lift the monstrous slab. Dory possessed incredible strength for a woman of her age. A musty stench stung my nostrils as I pushed aside a maze of cobwebs and switched on the light.

The figure of a black Cadillac appeared out of the

blackness. It was the same car I saw on Hillside Avenue. The garage door slammed as I stomped toward Dory's apartment and threw open the back door. "Dory!" I yelled, but there was no response. The place was dark except for a light above the kitchen stove. She was probably at Leary's Tavern, and I hurried to my truck as a light snow fell.

Dory was drinking a beer at the bar, with a half-empty martini glass next to her and two cigarettes burning in the ashtray. She had company and wasn't surprised to see me.

"You're not still mad at me, are you, Patrick?"

Shaking off the snow, I replied, "Was that your black Cadillac outside my old house last week?"

She considered the question for a moment, then answered. "Yes, I just wanted to see where you lived."

"Why did you drive away when I approached the car?"

"I was afraid you'd be angry at me again." Dory's face morphed into the Mask of Tragedy, and she switched subjects. "I tried to find Jim LaFrance through the Patrolman's Benevolent Association, but they didn't have an address for him. I've got something for you." Dory handed me a photograph of a man in a police uniform.

"That's him."

He looked like me at age twenty-nine. James LaFrance was the physical match to someone I thought was unique. That person was one of a kind, a bundle of cursed ambitions and talents who struggled to find success and acceptance in life. I'd never know if we shared more than just a bodily identity.

"He's dead," I said.

Dory's face dropped, and for once she was speechless.

"Do you know an ex-cop named John Darling? He confirmed that Jim LaFrance was my birth father."

"See, I told you the truth."

"That's the first time since I met you."

A woman with swirls of platinum hair and heavy makeup appeared from the back room. She walked over and wrinkled her eyebrows at me. "Patrick, you shouldn't treat your mother so rudely." Dory got up and moved next to the woman. I coughed from the smell of cigarette smoke and cheap perfume.

"Meet your Aunt Lana," said Dory.

Lana grabbed me in a bear hug and murmured how much she missed me, but it was pretentious and insincere. I tried to push her away, but she grabbed my face and

kissed me full on the lips. I tore away from her and used my sleeve to smear a blotch of ruby red lipstick off my mouth.

"It's good to finally meet you," gushed Lana. "You've made your poor mother so happy by coming back to her."

I studied Lana with curiosity and disgust. "Why did you call Howard Saltzman after forty years?"

"I wanted to surprise my sister and find you, but Mr. Saltzman refused to tell me anything. He was haughty." Lana moved next to Dory, and there was something familiar about them together.

"I met you both somewhere before," I said. "It was a long time ago."

They looked at each other and Dory asked, "Oh, where?"

She didn't say, *you couldn't have* or *how could that be?* Her response was, *where?*

"You stopped me on the street in Bedford when I was a child," I replied.

"Oh, that's impossible," insisted Lana. "I never laid eyes on you, and the last time your mother saw you was outside Redmond General, five days after your birth."

A flashback struck with no warning. *Two ladies bun-*

dled up in the middle of July, dripping with kindness and reaching for my hand.

"You both came for me in Bedford, didn't you?" I shouted. "Somehow you found me and stalked my family."

Dory lost her temper. "You have no proof of that! I did Eleanor and Artie a favor by letting them adopt my baby. They *owed* me!"

"They owed you nothing!" I yelled.

I turned to Lana. "You're a party to all of this. What do you have to say?"

She replied with a sinister laugh. Every drunk in the bar watched as Clyde ran over to referee the impending altercation. Without warning, Dory rushed at me yelling, "I'm going to shove you!" I winced at that word and turned to the side as Dory missed me and fell flat onto the floor. The place went wild.

People chanted, "Get up, Dory!" and clapped their hands in a frenzy. A carnival atmosphere echoed throughout the bar.

Clyde tried to help, but Lana tripped him and he fell on top of Dory. Lana whirled around and fell back against the bar, sending her martini glass crashing to the floor. Drunken spectators pulled Dory and Clyde to their feet as Lana lost her balance and slid to the floor with a thud. Three bar stools toppled over, knocking the blonde wig off her head. It was a comical yet pathetic scene.

The word *shove* always triggered the same involuntary quiver. When I was two years old, a woman's voice said, "I'm going to *shove* you!" moments before she pushed me down that flight of stairs. There was a connection between the hot shower and the fall down the stairs, the lady on the lawn in Redmond, and the two ladies on the street in Bedford. It was Dory and Lana.

I ran out of Leary's Tavern.

Easing my vehicle to the curb across from 27 Rogers Place, I parked and sat in the darkness. Once again, a vision appeared. This time the yard became illuminated, and the covering of snow melted away. It was much different than the previous flashbacks I'd experienced.

In great clarity, Dory inched toward the little boy on the lawn, and Eleanor snatched him up just in time. As Dory fled in a puff of smoke like some evil witch, I marveled at Eleanor's radiance. A vision of loveliness I knew only from photographs and not from real life. The beauty she possessed faded from the rabid visitations of a relentless birth mother who hungered for more money. Patrick suffered terrible injuries at the hands of Dory, and Eleanor wouldn't allow that to happen again. I'd witnessed a clear event from the past, and at last understood the sacrifices that Eleanor and Artie made to keep me safe.

———◇———

Tina looked worried. "Where were you?"

"Redmond," I answered. "Now I know what happened."

A ringing telephone interrupted me, and a man's voice warned, "Stop prying into police business or you'll end up dead. We know what you want and we won't give it to you." Before I could say anything, the nameless caller hung up. The color drained from my face as I looked at Tina. "That was a threat."

"Patrick, you have to end this now!" she cried.

Sergeant Wilson of the Redmond Police Department called with an update. "The investigation is generating more angry reactions from retired cops, and they're not just Redmond police officers. Some of these guys worked in the neighboring towns of Bloomfield, Montclair, and Hillside. They won't tell me why they're interested."

"I'm not surprised," I said. "One of them called and threatened me."

"Did you get his name?" asked Wilson.

"No, there wasn't enough time to ask. Why do these guys care about a kidnapping that happened forty years ago?"

"I don't know, but I'll find out."

"An ex-cop named John Darling called me to discuss Jim LaFrance. We met and he said I look like LaFrance, but I'm not convinced that was his true motivation for the meeting."

"There's a fraternal bond of protection among police officers," said Wilson. "They're hiding something, and we're getting close to uncovering the secret. My advice to you is lay low and stay away from them. I'll call you next week to meet and go over everything we have. Take care."

Tina listened to the entire conversation. "Patrick, don't you get the John Darling connection? Dory was running around with a bunch of cops, and Darling wanted to see if you were *his* son."

CHAPTER 12

A week passed, and no word from Sergeant Wilson. He promised to call in a few days to set up a meeting, and it concerned me. The Redmond desk sergeant answered the phone.

"What is this in reference to?"

"The Callahan investigation," I answered.

"All inquiries must be made to the city attorney."

"Why? What happened?"

"That's all I can tell you."

Eddie Snow offered an explanation. "They blocked you like a Nolan Ryan shutout. The investigation uncovered something incriminating and the Blue Wall of Silence came crashing down. I'll stop at the department tomorrow and see what I can find out, but I can't push it. They don't have to tell me anything."

"I'm going with you," I said.

On a chilly Monday morning, Eddie pulled his unmarked police car into the Redmond Municipal Complex. "You wait here," he instructed, and disappeared through a side entrance.

Sergeant Wilson ushered Eddie into the chief's office.

"You should drop your subterranean investigation now," said Chief Costello. "This proceeding doesn't concern you, and you're not here on official business."

"I'm here to help a friend."

"Yes, and your friend is Patrick Callahan. I understand his desire to uncover the past, but this thing is more complicated than that. Too many retired cops insisted that we stop searching through old incident reports, and we have to respect their right to privacy."

"They must have something big to hide," said Eddie.

"Word came down from the mayor's office to drop the investigation, and that's what we're doing."

Sergeant Wilson interrupted. "There's no incident report

related to the Callahans. That's what Patrick Callahan was looking for and we can't help him. End of story."

"I'm not so sure about that," countered Eddie.

"I don't like what you're saying," said Wilson. He curled his lip and stepped forward, but Chief Costello motioned for him to calm down.

"I'm saying this," said Eddie. "If there's no incident report, then there's nothing to worry about. Right, Wilson?"

"We have nothing more to say," stated the chief. "Sergeant Wilson – escort Investigator Snow out of the building."

An anxious Sergeant Wilson led Eddie Snow through police headquarters and out the exit door. "Snow, I have to talk to you," he said. The two men slipped behind a SWAT bus and I got out of the car to join them.

"Listen," said Wilson. "You're treading on dangerous ground."

"What do you mean?" asked Eddie.

"This thing is big and you've got to back off. That's all I can tell you. Back off!"

Sergeant Wilson bolted through a back door in the police station while Eddie and I stood there looking at each other.

"We've opened Pandora's Box," he remarked.

It was mid March and the winter cold lifted. Spring was a week away and I wanted to close the remaining chapter of my adoption saga. Rocky Manetti begged for one last chance to help me, and offered to drive me to the Newark Public Library for family research. I sat on the front porch waiting for the tan Mercedes convertible to pull up.

Severe pain pierced my lower back as I shifted in agony. A recent back problem exposed the full extent of my childhood injuries.

Earlier in the week, I'd lifted a heavy spool of wire and a sharp pain shot up my spine. This happened while I was wiring an addition on a chiropractor's office, and the doctor helped me into his exam room for treatment. He took several x-rays of my lower back, spinal column, and neck and examined the negatives.

"Were you in a car wreck as a young child?" he asked. "Or did you jump from a swing set at a high elevation and land squarely on your feet?"

"No. Why, doctor?"

The chiropractor pointed to several points along the

spinal column. "These are healed fractures of the T4 and T5 thoracic vertebrae in your back, and C5 and C6 cervical vertebrae in your neck. They're old injuries you suffered as a child."

I asked him to look at the creases in my eyebrows.

"They're scars," he concluded. "What happened to you?"

He confirmed the trauma I suffered at the hands of Dory. I dragged myself off the exam table and said, "It dawned on me. I took a bad spill as a toddler."

A Crown Victoria chugged up the street with Rocky in the driver's seat. "Hurry!" he yelled. "I don't want to shut it off!"

I hobbled out to the street and hesitated getting into the car. "It's okay," said Rocky. "She has to warm up a little bit. The Mercedes is still in the repair shop. It needs a transmission."

I groaned in pain and climbed into the wreck of a car.

"Say, Pasquale, are you okay? You're limping around like an old man."

"It's nothing," I replied. "Just a little back problem. Who owns the Mercedes Benz?"

He looked at me like a naughty puppy. "One of my rich widow clients. It's her second car."

We cruised down the highway at twenty-five miles an hour, with a line of traffic backed up behind us. Rocky pulled into the first tollbooth on the Garden State Parkway and turned to me.

"Say, got any change?"

I cursed and dug into my pocket.

We survived the trip to Newark, and the car shimmied like a washing machine as it came to rest in the public parking lot. Rocky followed me up the library steps.

"Hold on," he said.

"What?" I asked.

Rocky looked up to the sky and raised his hand. I heard a cannon blast, and several pedestrians hit the ground in fear. It was just the sound of the car backfiring.

"Okay, she's off," announced Rocky.

I asked the librarian for the *Essex County News* microfilm list, and she pointed to a card catalog. Rocky gave her a lustful stare and remarked, "You are a beautiful lady." The librarian laughed. I rolled my eyes and walked away.

There was no listing for Callahan or Sochek, but I found a 1950 wedding announcement for James La-France. We waited for the microfilm, and Rocky leaned over the counter like a rabid hound dog. He whispered from the corner of his mouth. "I think she's ready to give me her phone number."

"I thought you were dating Dory," I said sarcastically.

"Nah, she's got expensive taste. One meal in a restaurant cost me over a hundred bucks. She's nice, but she ain't *that* nice."

"You're unbelievable," I said.

Rocky grinned, "Ain't I, though?" He laughed and pulled a comb from his back pocket, primping himself for the librarian's return. I never mentioned the incident at Leary's Tavern with Dory and Lana; he would've placed the blame on me. Dory hadn't contacted me since.

Marietta Siciliano and James LaFrance were joined in Holy Matrimony on April 25th, 1950. That was the opening sentence of the article. The newlyweds moved into a new home at 10 Newhope Road in Redmond, and the story included a photograph of raven-haired Marietta and twenty-three-year-old James LaFrance. Our resemblance was astounding. I wondered if Marietta was still alive and living at the same address.

"Come on," I said to Rocky. "We have to go."

The overheated car ground to a halt at 10 Newhope Road.

"I'll leave it running," said Rocky.

"You do that," I replied. The car door creaked as I got out, and my back was aching more than ever. It was a difficult climb up the concrete steps, but worth the trip when I saw a mailbox with the name "LaFrance" written in brushstroke.

The doorbell echoed throughout the house, and a man close to my age opened the door and asked, "Can I help you?" He had dark hair and looked like me. It caught me off guard.

"My name is Patrick Callahan. I'm the son of James LaFrance."

A look of confusion, then suspicion, covered the man's face. "How?" he asked.

"Can I come inside to explain? Please, I'm not crazy."

He thought for a moment, then stepped aside to allow me entry. As I passed him, we took a long look at each other and registered the same thought...*we were sons of the same father*.

"I'm James LaFrance, Jr," he said.

As soon as I entered the living room, a pretty young woman with auburn hair stopped short when she saw my face.

"Bridget," said James. "This is Patrick Callahan. He claims to be our father's son."

"My God," she exclaimed. "You look like him. Where did you come from?"

"It's a long story," I answered.

James and Bridget didn't know how to react to my sudden appearance. Bridget seemed nervous and James was tense and apprehensive.

"What do you want from us?" he asked.

"Information about your father," I replied. "I want to know if he tried to find me. Did Jim have any medical conditions?"

"Just alcoholism," replied James. "He never said that I had a half-brother."

"It was news to me, too. I was raised as an only child."

Bridget gave James a sympathetic look, and his tightened features relaxed.

"Please have a seat," said Bridget.

I settled on the couch, and she never took her tearful

eyes off of me. James stood next to her as I told them the story of Dory and Jim. It didn't surprise James at all.

"Our father cheated on mother from the beginning, and it caused her a lot of heartache. He was an ex-cop with anger issues and a penchant for alcohol.

"James LaFrance had no interest in us; he only cared about the fast women he met in taverns and seedy hotels. My mother threw him out when we were little, and they divorced when I was five and Bridget was three.

"He picked us up once a month to visit the park or go to the movies, but we always ended up at a bar in Newark. Our father sat inside drinking whiskey and beer while Bridget and I ran around the parking lot."

"It was so sad," remarked Bridget.

With that, an old woman with a cane appeared in the doorway. Her classic Italian features were striking, accented by a cloud of snow white hair. Piercing eyes fixed on me as she spoke.

"Why have you come here to bother me?"

"Are you Marietta LaFrance?" I asked.

"You don't answer a question with a question!"

"Mom, please," interrupted James. "This is Patrick Callahan. He claims to be our brother."

"Yes, I heard," said Marietta.

James Jr. took his mother's arm and led her to a wing-back chair. Marietta sat down and placed both hands on top of her cane.

"You look just like my ex-husband," remarked Marietta. "It's quite astounding." She leaned forward and frowned. "I hope you don't have the same bad habits as him."

"No," I replied. "I don't."

"Good. Do you have a family?"

"Yes. I have a wife and daughter."

"Take care of them."

"What can you tell me about my birth father?" I asked.

Marietta studied me. "I can tell you plenty. Do you want to hear the full story?"

"Yes," I replied.

Marietta told me that Jim LaFrance was the youngest child of Dutch and Irish immigrants. His father, Jack La-France, was a French Huguenot orphan born in Rotterdam, Holland on October 29, 1906, fifty years to the day before me. Jack was an artistic bon vivant and a ladies man. He left his wife and children behind many times to travel the world with various female companions and sell his paintings.

Bridget O'Neill was a lovely young woman from County Clare, Ireland, and the namesake of Marietta's daughter. She met the dashing Jack LaFrance at a Newark, New Jersey dance hall and they soon married.

When Jim was a teenager, Bridget contracted cancer. Not to be burdened with an ailing wife and four children, Jack promptly abandoned his family, never to return.

After Jack's disappearance, young Jim folded to the pressure of attending to his younger sisters and sick mother. He lied about his age and joined the navy at age seventeen during the Second World War. Bridget and the girls moved into a home for the poor.

While on a ship crossing the Pacific Ocean, Jim LaFrance received word that his mother had died. He never forgave himself for running off and leaving Bridget behind, and suffered from a burning self-hatred for the rest of his life. Although he was as charming as his father Jack, Jim grew into a bitter and angry man.

Marietta spoke of their rocky marriage and described Jim as a violent, drunken womanizer who cheated on her from the moment they married. She planned to leave him after the birth of their son, but he begged her to stay. Marietta became pregnant with Bridget, and life continued in the same fashion.

One day, Marietta received a call from a prostitute named Dory Sochek, who claimed that she was carrying Jim LaFrance's child. He came home late that night in a drunken rage, and a violent argument ensued. Marietta threw him out for good, and the police force discharged LaFrance for threatening the prostitute. From that day on, he had little contact with Marietta and the children.

"Dory Sochek is my birth mother," I said.

"Ironic, isn't it?" said Marietta. "You were born of Jim's affair, and now here you are sitting in my living room."

"I had no choice," I said, and turned away.

James LaFrance Jr. sensed my despair and disappeared into the other room. He returned carrying an old shoebox that looked like Artie's last keepsake.

"Here are my father's personal possessions," said James. "It's not much, but you might like to have it. I was never close to my father, so maybe you can find something of value in this box of photographs and journals."

The sound of a car horn shattered the moment.

"That's my ride," I said. "He's a little impatient."

I thanked the LaFrance family for their honesty and

left the house. The Crown Victoria waited for me at curbside.

"Hey, what took you so long?" asked Rocky.

I got into the car and said, "I was using *psycho-logee* on them."

A blank expression covered Rocky's face, until he noticed the shoebox on my lap, then he smiled.

"See, it works!"

While Rocky's car limped toward the parkway, I sorted through Jim LaFrance's belongings. There were three well-documented journals, an address book, and several photographs.

An antique sepia postcard depicted a young male artist standing at his easel with a paint palette in hand. Seated in a nearby chair was a stunning model. The artist shared the same features as Jim LaFrance and me. Writing on the reverse side read: "Jack LaFrance painting a portrait of Bridget O'Neill,1925." Now I knew where my artistic talents came from…Jack LaFrance. He was a true Dutch artist.

The car engine sounded more distressed than usual. We were in the center lane approaching the Raritan River

Bridge, and Rocky wore an expression of fear.

"Don't panic!" I yelled, reciting Rocky's famous line.

"We're almost out of gas!" he cried.

"Didn't you fill the tank before we left?"

"No. I didn't have enough money."

"What about the five hundred bucks I gave you?"

"Oh, that's all gone."

I wanted to strangle him. We sat on needles as the Crown Victoria coughed and belched its way up to the crest of the bridge. We were destined to stall out in the middle of the parkway at rush hour.

"Move over to the right lane!" I bellowed. "We have to get to the shoulder when the car stalls out!"

Rocky thought for a second. "I got an idea. If we both lean forward, we can get enough motion to push the car over the hill."

"Are you crazy?" I asked.

"Come on!" "It's worth a try!"

He pitched his body toward the dashboard to coerce the junk heap forward. Out of desperation, I followed Rocky's lead. The car was choking out fumes from an empty gas tank as both of my hands gripped the dashboard and pushed with all my strength. I prayed for a miracle as the car limped over the crown of the bridge and finally conked out.

Rocky slammed the gearshift into neutral and coasted downhill, right through the toll plaza. Bells went off to signal non-payment as we rolled onto a nearby ramp and into a large parking lot. The car ground to a halt in front of a gas pump with a waiting attendant. Rocky shifted the gear into park and turned to me with a proud grin.

"I told you we'd make it. You got ten bucks?"

The only satisfaction I got out of the adventure came when a New Jersey State Trooper cruised up in his patrol car to write Rocky a summons for running the toll plaza.

March 17th, 1997 – St. Patrick's Day. It was a Callahan family tradition to gather at Aunt Peggy's house each year to celebrate our national holiday. The day of revel included music, corned beef and cabbage, potatoes, soda bread, and plenty of beer.

At the culmination of the party, The Sisters formed a chorus line and sang "Callahan" to the tune of "Harrigan." Artie looked forward to this celebration every March, right up to the year he died. He sat on Aunt Peggy's couch one last time in 1994, smiling at the festivities through an oxygen mask.

Everything changed in March 1995, when Aunt Peggy reported that the tradition ended due to lack of interest, age, and illness. "You have Tina now," she said, echoing Aunt Joanie's classic line. So we started our own observance that year and hosted a St. Patrick's Day party at home. The Sisters declined the offer.

In 1997, vacations and family obligations depleted our guest list and we canceled the party. I accepted an invitation to a friend's house in Bedford and passed by Aunt Peggy's place on the way. I heard Irish music and slowed down.

The sound of bagpipes filled the air and familiar cars lined Aunt Peggy's driveway. I walked up to the sprawling ranch and saw my aunts and uncles sitting at picnic tables, applauding the pipe band. Age and illness hadn't restricted them in the least. They ate, drank, and laughed like teenagers. The entire Callahan Clan was present at this St. Patrick's Day celebration, every Callahan except me. I returned to the car.

"That's just plain lousy, Patrick," said Tina.

"Yup," I replied. "It's over."

CHAPTER 13

Mulligan's Pub was crowded that Saturday night, and the tall figure of Hughie the bartender appeared through the stained glass window. He waved both arms over his head like an airport runway attendant in a puzzling dance, and I didn't know what he was trying to tell me. I walked in with Tina and spotted Dory and Lana seated at the bar. It was too late to turn away, and Hughie shook his head. "I tried to warn you."

"My God," exclaimed Tina. "What are they doing here?"

"Oh, Patrick," mused Dory. "I asked around town and they told me this was your hangout. We like Hughie the bartender. He gave us a free drink."

"We came here for a week straight hoping to see you," added Lana.

I hurried Tina to a nearby booth and she gave me a desperate look. "You can't allow them to do this to us! Tell Dory to leave!"

"Let me find out what they want," I said.

"Money, to make them go away for now."

Dory sat in the booth next to me. She smiled at Tina and I glared back at her like a protective lion.

"What do you want?" I snapped.

"I'm glad you're back in my life, Patrick. You have a beautiful family and a successful business. When I look at your face, I see Jim LaFrance."

I had fire in my eyes. "Stay away from us! You won't repeat what you did to my parents."

Dory gave me an innocent look. "I don't know what you're talking about, Patrick. I did nothing to your parents and I'd never harm you."

Tina shot up and shouted, "Let's get out of here!" as we bolted toward the door. Lana gave me a sardonic smile as she sipped her martini, and Hughie snatched the glass from her hand and dumped it into the bar sink. "You're both done," he commanded.

Lana McGovern lived on Lorraine Drive in Toms River, and I arrived that Monday morning. It was a decrepit house surrounded by junk cars, broken birdbaths, and a vintage motor home with three flat tires. Lana was a repulsive woman, but I had to talk to her alone.

Wooden steps creaked under my feet as I climbed past two abandoned refrigerators on the back porch. Bundles of old magazines were stacked six feet tall on either side of a rotted wooden door. I rapped on the doorframe, fearing that the puttied panes of glass might fall out.

A pasty Lana peered through smudged glass, squinting in the glaring sun. Her dark sunken eyes greeted me and a Cheshire smile curled her lips. The door opened and acrid smoke emanated from within. Lana lingered in the doorway with a cigarette hanging from her mouth.

"Patrick, I knew you'd come."

The kitchen table and countertop was a maze of books, magazines, and ragged notebooks crammed full of browned sheets of paper. Ancient scrawled notes littered every surface. Lana was a crazed packrat.

"Have a seat," she said.

There was nowhere to sit. Every chair had boxes

of newspaper clippings and issues of the *National Geographic* piled high. Lana took note, swung a crate of paperwork off the chair, and slammed it to the floor. She ordered me to sit.

"Patrick, you upset your mother at Mulligan's Pub the other night. Not to mention the incident at Leary's Tavern."

My eyes focused on her mock disapproval. "She deserves to be upset for not telling me the truth about my adoption and the aftermath. There's more to it than that, and that's why I'm here. What do you both want from me?"

Lana maintained a straight face and said, "We want you to be happy."

I laughed. "Let's be honest. You're after something."

"We want to be a part of your life. That attorney robbed your poor mother forty years ago."

"She gave me up."

Another box of paperwork hit the floor and Lana sat down.

"You have questions," observed Lana. "Shoot."

"Okay, how is it you never found me when we live fifteen minutes apart?"

"It was an oversight. I searched with no luck."

I peered at her with narrow eyes. "You're too smart for that. Be honest, did you find me?"

Lana sipped her coffee and took a drag of the cigarette. "How intuitive you are." The ear-splitting ring of a specialized kitchen phone prompted her to adjust two large hearing aids and answer it in a loud voice, "Susan! Your cousin Patrick showed up at my doorstep and I'm thrilled to death!" She stretched the cord into the dining room to chat with her daughter in private.

A bundle of address books caught my attention, tied together with brittle string that snapped under my fingers. Each book contained dates from 1956 to 1960, testifying that all roads led back to those crucial years. Like Dory's photographic hospital record, Lana chronicled the phone numbers of every person involved since my birth.

She saved the phone numbers and addresses for Howard Saltzman, Billy Van Winkle, and Jim LaFrance. It was proof that Lana contacted Dory's people. Eleanor and Artie Callahan didn't make the list, but there was another entry in the 1960 address book under the "C" section, *Joan and Harry Croft, 1610 Walton Street, Bedford.* That was the link between Dory, Lana, and my parents. Lana hurried back to the kitchen as if radar went off in her head.

"How do you know Joan and Harry Croft?" I demanded.

"Oh, they were friends of mine from Newark," she explained. "They moved down here the same time as me."

"In 1960. They were my neighbors."

"Really? I used to visit them all the time." Lana chuckled. "That falls under the 'small world' category by pure coincidence."

"There's nothing coincidental about it. It's a lie. You knew that we lived right down the street."

Lana laughed. "You can't prove that."

I held up the address book. "The proof is right here, and I'm taking it with me."

"That's mine!" screamed an infuriated Lana. She lunged at me and tried to snatch the book as I whipped past her. Lana pounded on my back as I flew through the back door and the window putty gave way. Glass shattered onto the back porch, and Lana shuffled through it, cackling like a mental patient.

I peeled down Lorraine Drive with a car following me. It was a 1960 dark blue vintage Impala with blacked-out windows gaining speed. I accelerated and took a few sharp turns to see if it was my imagination, but the Impala tailed me. *Who the hell was it?* I sped toward the highway with the car on my rear bumper.

The Impala rammed my truck at the highway intersection and pushed me into oncoming traffic. Blasting horns and swerving cars forced me to squeeze in and floor the gas pedal. The Impala screamed out behind me and rammed the rear bumper a second time. In desperation, I crossed the double solid line into oncoming traffic, and a box truck veered around me. I darted back into my lane with three cars between the pursuer and me.

A police car traveling in the opposite direction screeched on its brakes. The officer flipped on the lights and siren and whipped around to pull me over, just as the Impala crossed over the line. He raced head-on toward the police cruiser, and the officer swerved in time to avoid a collision. The cop pulled the Impala over on the shoulder and I blended into a maze of cars.

I sat breathless in my driveway, expecting a squad of police cars to come screaming down the street, but they never did. The ordeal was over for now.

The incident didn't surprise Eddie Snow at all. "Your interrogation methods are putting you in danger. You have to stop questioning these people."

"Can't the prosecutor investigate the brothel and baby-selling ring?" I asked. "It's all tied together."

"Those events happened long ago and there's no benefit in bringing it to the surface now. Like Sergeant Wilson said, this thing is big."

"So, that's it?"

"I spoke to the prosecutor and he wants no part of it. Sorry, Pat."

On a balmy spring afternoon, I took Tina and Clare for a drive. Life was calm again. Dory went into seclusion, and I stayed away from Redmond. The threatening calls and high-speed chases stopped, and Dory and Lana never returned to Mulligan's Pub. My search came to a grinding halt.

I was interested in home and family and work once again, and I became a better husband and father. The full details of my adoption remained concealed, and I learned to accept that reality. Perhaps it was for the best.

Warm fresh air breezed through the open car windows. Tina was smiling and Clare giggled as a butterfly danced across her face. The long, cold winter was over. My business flourished, and Tina booked a vacation to the Bahamas. We needed a relaxing week in the sun with Clare, far from New Jersey and the dark events of the past year.

"Isn't this your old neighborhood?" asked Tina.

We were driving down Lexington Road in Bedford. "Yes," I replied. "It must have been subconscious."

House number 2709 was the same two-bedroom ranch I called home from the age of four to sixteen. Eleanor's blue shutters and flower boxes still accented the front windows. Years of settling fractured the concrete porch where I played with my toy trucks and army men.

"Ooh!" cried Clare. "Swings!"

Clare pointed to a playground behind the house. It was once a lush wooded hideaway where I spent many childhood hours building tree forts. I came home from school on a spring afternoon like today to find my precious woods mowed down and replaced with a merry-go-round, swing sets, and monkey bars.

"Let's take Clare to the playground and push her on the swings," said Tina.

"Sure," I answered. "Walk her over. I'll be right there."

Tina marched Clare across the yard toward the park and motioned to my former home. Clare exclaimed, "Daddy's house!" I was enjoying the moment when a sharp rap on the doorframe startled me. It was Rose Larkin, former neighbor and Eleanor's only friend.

"Are you looking for someone?" demanded Rose. She didn't recognize me in dark sunglasses, so I took them off and smiled.

"Yes," I said. "I'm looking for you."

"Patrick!" exclaimed Rose. She reached through the open car window and hugged me. "How are you?"

"I'm doing well."

Rose looked at the playground. "Is that your wife and daughter?"

"Yes. Tina and Clare."

"Beautiful."

We reminisced about the old days in Bedford, and Rose lamented the loss of Eleanor, Artie, and her husband Phil. The Larkins befriended my parents and remained close until the day we moved.

Rose admitted that she knew about my adoption, and Eleanor begged her to keep it a secret. Even though my mother suffered a bad experience, she encouraged Rose to adopt three children of her own, and Rose was grateful for that.

"Eleanor warned me to adopt through a proper agency," said Rose. "She didn't want me to go through the same hell."

"Tell me about the trouble, Rose."

She folded her arms and looked toward the sky, searching for a heavenly answer. There was only one option, and that was honesty. "Eleanor made a deal with the devil. She didn't give me details, but I knew your adoption was black market. Your parents moved here to get away from those people in north Jersey. Eleanor never uttered their names, but I knew it was your birth mother and her sister."

"Dory and Lana," I said.

"They're bad people, Patrick. Those women befriended the Croft family and called your mother every day. They stalked the neighborhood and hid in the woods behind your house to spy on you. Dory tried to grab you off the school bus, but I stopped her.

"Flora and Willy made monthly payments to an attorney up north, but that didn't stop your birth mother from extorting money from Eleanor and Artie. They borrowed thousands from friends and family, and that woman wasted it. Willy told your father to stop paying her and it drove poor Eleanor mad. Then Flora and Willy died and Eleanor lost their support."

Rose reopened the nearly-healed wound. I covered my face and said, "It's tragic." Her hand was on my shoulder, and it took a few minutes to compose myself.

"Did Dory scald me in a hot shower?" I asked.

Rose gave a pained expression and tears streamed from her eyes as she acknowledged the tragedy. "We hoped it wasn't intentional. She was drunk and tried to bathe you."

I looked at Rose and said, "Dory shoved me down a flight of stairs." She turned away and bit her lip at the news.

I watched Tina push Clare on the swings and thought of Eleanor and Artie. With a distant tone, I uttered the words, "I miss my parents."

Rose smiled and said, "The tree is gone, but the roots are still there."

CHAPTER 14

It was late April 1997 when I visited a small garden apartment complex in the shore town of Brielle. The Rose Larkin conversation rekindled my adoption investigation, and Tina wasn't happy about it, but I had to take this to the very end. I rang the doorbell to the first floor unit and waited.

"This is a surprise," said John Darling. "How did you find me?"

"We share the same auto mechanic in Manasquan. Can we talk?"

Darling nodded and invited me in. His home was neat and well furnished.

"Would you like something to drink?" he asked.

"No thanks," I replied. "I want to ask you about our meeting at the Pinnacle Diner. There's another reason why you wanted to see me."

"No other reason. I was curious to see if you resembled Jim LaFrance, that's all."

"That's only partly true. You needed to know if I looked like you. It was obvious that I was the child of Jim LaFrance and you tried to slip away."

Darling studied me. "I had a short tryst with Dory Sochek and suspected you might be my son. You're right, and I apologize for that."

I gave him a stern look. "If I've learned anything from this entire ordeal, it's the fact that everyone acted on their own selfish needs. That's what this is all about; no one is capable of telling the truth. You got yourselves into this mess with no way out."

John Darling nodded and said, "If I had the sense to think that way, I'd still be married. In my defense, I was part of a dark underworld of police corruption and street thieves. Most of the force participated in that lifestyle for so long it became our normal. That's not an excuse, just a fact."

"Tell me about you, Dory, and Jim," I said.

Darling pointed to a pair of chairs in the living room and we sat down. Then he spoke.

"Back in January of 1956, Jim and I frequented a Redmond brothel on Main Street with other cops in Essex County. Dory and Lana worked there, and we discovered that Howard Saltzman ran it as a baby mill.

"Dory was pregnant and showed up at McDonnell's Tavern in Newark, where I hung out with Jim LaFrance. She pestered Jim, claiming it was his child and demanded money from both of us. I suspected that the baby might be mine, and we told her to get lost.

"That crazy woman flagged down my patrol car the next day and said she exposed the affair to our wives. Jim LaFrance was enraged, and he jumped out of the car and put a gun to Dory's head. The department filed attempted murder charges and fired Jim from the police force. Then we both got divorced." Darling laughed. "Jim was a great guy, but he was crazy. They reassigned me to the Hillside Police Department and I never saw Jim LaFrance again."

"Dory pulled the same pregnancy scam on a man named Billy Van Winkle," I said.

"Lonesome Billy," noted Darling. "He always sat in the corner of McDonnell's Tavern moping. Billy was the scrawny, timid type."

"So that's where Dory met Billy. Saltzman named him as my birth father in a falsified adoption record, and Dory blackmailed Billy for years."

"Van Winkle was a patsy, just like Lee Harvey Oswald," said Darling. "LaFrance would've killed Dory if she put his name on that adoption file. That's why she used Van Winkle instead."

"Billy died earlier this year," I added.

"Free at last," quipped Darling.

"What do you know about my kidnapping?"

Darling was hesitant to talk about it. He wrestled with his conscience for a few seconds and gazed at a photograph of himself as a young Redmond police officer.

"Dory arranged to meet with Eleanor Callahan at a luncheonette to lure her away from home," began Darling. "Eleanor's mother babysat, and Lana knocked on the door pretending to be a census taker. She grabbed you and fled to Dory's apartment, where Dory hurt you.

"Your parents called the police and they arrested Dory and Lana. Two cops brought you home, but you had to be rushed to the hospital for your injuries. Howard Saltzman used his position to cover up the incident and your parents disappeared." John Darling looked me straight in the eyes. "Now you know the truth."

I sat in horrified silence as Darling related the story. Lana was the kidnapper, and she delivered me into the evil arms of Dory Sochek. My brain pounded with one sickening question, *how could a mother do that to her own child?* It was unthinkable, unimaginable, and inhuman, and worst of all, it was true.

Eleanor must have suffered from terrible guilt, and feared that her child might be injured again. Dory unleashed a relentless campaign of terror against the woman who adopted her child, and it was all for money. Eleanor succumbed to the pressure in a tragic irony of good versus evil and birth mother versus adoptive mother. She numbed the pain with prescription medication. I tried to accept the chilling facts without falling apart.

A manila envelope arrived at my house via Lawyers Delivery Service. It came from a law firm in Princeton, New Jersey, and contained copies of Eleanor's medical records from the Waverly Rehabilitation Clinic. I'd sent for them hoping to learn more about her treatment, and the mysterious visits to the clinic with Artie.

Artie took me to Waverly in the summer of 1967, and sneaked me inside through a service entrance. I sat in the arts and crafts room, and the kind instructor gave me clay and modeling tools for entertainment.

I was sculpting an action figure when the door opened, and Artie led Eleanor into the room. She wore a blue bathrobe and a beaming smile, looking thoroughly medicated. Eleanor leaned forward and kissed me. "Hi, Pat," she said. "What brings you here?"

We talked for a few minutes, until Artie told her it was time to go. "I'll be back soon," he said, as the door closed behind them. My mother was a stranger to me.

The microfilm copies were faint and difficult to read, but they told the story of Eleanor Callahan's stay at Waverly Clinic. It was a sad story, and the closing sentences floored me.

"The patient is severely depressed, due to the fact that she is unable to have children. She lives alone with her husband."

It was an unimaginable blow to my entire sense of being. Eleanor and Artie denied my existence and status as their son, and I walked outside to catch my breath. Tina followed and put her arm around my waist. She'd read the page I dropped onto the kitchen counter, and knew it contained the most hurtful news of all.

"They did it to keep you out of foster care," she said.

Docket Number 7685 was stamped on the upper right corner of the Judgment of Adoption. By all accounts, my adoption was illegal and I was a product of the black market. I had to know for certain if Saltzman filed falsified documents with the Essex County Court. The rush of pedestrians and noise from the street traffic faded as I climbed the pyramid-like steps leading to the front entrance of the building.

A throng of people crowded the elevator, and the pungent odor of perfume, cologne, and cigarettes pervaded the enclosed space. I held my breath for the sixty-second ascent. The crowd crushed through the open door, and I found myself in a long hallway.

"Can I help you?" asked the Family Court clerk.

"Yes," I replied. "I'd like to know if my adoption papers are legitimate."

She gave me a strange look and took the onion-skinned adoption papers from my hand. "Hmmm, this is unusual. Where did you get these?"

"From the adoption attorney."

"I'll be right back," said the clerk. "The judge is in his chambers. I want to ask him about this." She disappeared behind a heavy wooden door and returned moments later. "Mr. Callahan, will you please have a seat in the waiting area? I have to go to our records room."

The clerk returned with a blue file folder and re-entered the judge's chambers. I waited in a cold sweat with my eyes locked on the closed door. She found something in the file, and the judge had enough interest to review the sealed document. The fate of my entire investigation was in their hands, along with the legitimacy of my adoption. A voice called my name.

"Mr. Callahan – Judge Brennan wishes to see you."

Judge Brennan had the look of a Kennedy, and wore a serious expression. "We have an unusual situation, Mr. Callahan. You submitted an adoption file with docket number 7685, and I'm surprised an attorney gave this to you. It's a confidential document that's unsealed only through a court order signed by me. The original document should be on file in this courthouse. You'll notice I said, *should be*.

The judge held up the blue file folder. "This file is numbered 7685 and carries the marking: 'Callahan Adoption.' I just unsealed it, and there's one problem." Judge Brennan opened the folder and there was nothing inside.

"There is no adoption complaint, testimony from your adoptive parents, or letters of release from your biological parents. The question is, *who* filed this blank folder and *why?* Do you understand what I'm driving at, Mr. Callahan?"

I swallowed hard and said, "This wasn't a legal adoption."

"Exactly. This was made to *look* like a legal adoption. The charade would've continued for another forty years if not for your curiosity. I'm aware of Mr. Saltzman's questionable reputation, and accusations of impropriety have surfaced in the past, but this action involved guardians of the court. Even though four decades has passed, it still doesn't condone the behavior of the individuals responsible."

"I understand, your honor," I said. "Where does that leave me now?"

"I'm afraid it leaves you in limbo. The Callahans didn't legally adopt you, and charges of fraud must be filed against Howard Saltzman. Are you willing to do that?"

———— ‹◇› ————

My last name wasn't Callahan, it was Sochek. After forty years, Dory still had a hold on me, if only in name. The Sisters knew that and rejected me in every way possible. Artie always said I needed a brick wall to fall in on me before I accepted the facts, and that wall had fallen.

I found myself back on the streets of Newark, numbed by the news and standing before the Hall of Records building. It beckoned me into a marbled hallway with a sign that read, "Title and Deed Room."

The place was massive and full of leather-bound books. Groups of title clerks scurried about the room pulling deed books and dropping them onto tables. A line of people ran off copies on a nearby printer. I stood in the middle of the room not knowing why I was there when young man bumped into me and exclaimed, "Hey, you're in the way! What're you looking for?"

I said the first thing that popped into my head, "The title to my parents' house."

"I need a block and lot!" he snapped. "Amateur."

"Block two-thirty-seven-point-nine; lot ten," I blurted.

The clerk pulled a deed book off the shelf and ushered me to a table like a lost schoolboy. I leafed through the heavy tome and found 3 Hillside Avenue on page 2612. Arthur J. Callahan purchased the home on a VA loan in 1953, and the bank foreclosed in December 1958 after we abandoned the house. It was what I expected.

Three pages later, I found Dory's apartment building at 13 Summit Avenue. Only one person owned that property since 1951 . . . Howard R. Saltzman.

CHAPTER 15

I stormed into Howard Saltzman's law office and de-manded to see him. Before the secretary reacted, the aged attorney stepped out of his private quarters. Intuition told him the game was over.

"It's all right, Margaret. Come inside, Patrick."

I flew into the office and slammed the door behind me. "I know everything now! The court has no record of my adoption, and I was a product of the brothel on Main Street. Dory Sochek extorted money from my parents, and you allowed it to continue. You sold me!"

Saltzman slumped into a chair and raised his hand to calm me down. "Sit down, please." I dropped into an easy chair and slammed my briefcase to the floor. Saltzman composed himself and searched for the right words to say. I tried to read the language of his breathing. He inhaled with a hint of frustration and anxiety, and slowly exhaled with a mix of regret, confidence, and conviction. Saltzman took a slight pause and spoke.

"Eleanor and Artie shared a great love story, and Artie planned to spend a childless lifetime with Eleanor. However, after ten years of marriage, Eleanor longed for a child. She applied to Catholic Charities and Children's Services to adopt, but the agencies denied the applications because of Artie's disability. That's when Eleanor sought my help without Artie's knowledge.

"Dory worked in the brothel, and I knew she was carrying a child. I arranged a backdoor adoption, but it fell apart when Dory demanded a lot of money. Eleanor begged Elsie to give her the mother's name, and Eleanor went to Dory and pleaded with her to go through with the deal. She made a fatal mistake by revealing her identity.

"We used Connie Taylor as the contact person, and William Van Winkle as the biological father. The volatile James LaFrance was the probable birth father, but I chose to leave him out of it for obvious reasons.

"I concocted a series of events leading up to your adoption, and my secretary typed up the falsified documents to dissuade the curious. A judge on the payroll signed the order, and the clerk filed an empty adoption folder.

"Dory saw the Callahans as her meal ticket out of poverty, and launched an extortion plot to keep her silence. She forced Van Winkle to help until he broke free, and Lana McGovern picked up from there. I bought Dory a used black 1950 Cadillac as an appeasement, and pleaded with her to leave the couple alone. She refused, and threatened to go to the authorities and bring me down.

"Eleanor and Artie borrowed money from family and friends to pay Dory, and alienated everyone close to them. Dory and Lana kidnapped and harmed you, but that was out of my control. They wasted all that money on high living, parties, and alcohol.

"In 1958, I moved Dory into my apartment building on Summit Avenue to keep her quiet. By that time, your parents disappeared and I never saw them again."

"Why didn't you tell me this at the beginning?" I asked.

"I tried to shield you from the terrible truth, Patrick," answered Saltzman. "I gave you the adoption file thinking you'd go away happy, not knowing you're a tenacious bulldog."

———— ‹◇› ————

That night I couldn't sleep. Something still nagged at me. There had to be a connection between my birth family and my adoptive family. Tina was expecting our second child and I didn't want to wake her, so I slipped out of bed and went to my office to think.

Lana's McGovern's address book sat on the desk. Something told me to leaf through the remaining pages one more time, and there it was. The last link I was looking for. I jolted upright with my eyes glued to the page.

It was two o'clock in the morning when I picked up the phone and dialed the number. Someone picked up on the other end of the line and I said, "I know what you did."

CHAPTER 16

Later that morning, I took one last trip to Redmond. The full story of my adoption replayed in my head as I drove up the Garden State Parkway.

The search was over. Six months had passed since that cold November morning when I first heard the news. I'd taken a journey of self-discovery and re-discovery, and became a much stronger person than before. Now there was one last thing to do: I had to settle the score with Dory for myself, and Eleanor and Artie.

I entered Dory's apartment at ten-thirty in the morning and walked into the kitchen. As usual, Dory sat with a cigarette in one hand and a beer in the other. She knew it was the end by my dour expression.

"Patrick," she uttered. "Did something happen?"

"I had a serious talk with Howard Saltzman."

Dory hung her head. "I know. He called me this time."

"I have one question: when Lana kidnapped me, did you scald me and push me down those stairs on purpose? You said, 'I'm going to shove you.'"

Dory looked up at me with a pitiful face and said, "No, it was an accident. I was drunk and didn't mean it."

Rose Larkin was correct, and Dory's confession melted my anger to a state of extreme sadness. It was a tragic end to a sordid tale of lies, corruption, greed, and abuse. I looked into Dory's hollow eyes and said, "Don't ever come near my family again."

"Dory looked up at me with a pitiful face..."

CHAPTER 17

In the middle of May 2003, Tina and I threw a belated party for our tenth wedding anniversary. It was a gathering of family and friends at our Spring Lake Heights home, and we welcomed the day with great joy. Clare was seven years old, and happy to have a four-year-old sister named Katy.

Artie died nine years before, and it was a comfort to know that he reunited with his beloved Eleanor. He'd be happy to see I'd installed central air-conditioning in our home, and the intense heat and sadness of his repast evolved into the cool comfort of a happy celebration.

The business phone rang in my office, and the answering machine picked up. It was Sunday, and I thought it might be an emergency call, so I excused myself to retrieve the message. A familiar voice blasted from the speaker. "Hey, it's Rocky! I finally figured out that Billy Van Winkle was your real father. Sorry he's dead. It came to me in a dream."

I laughed and gazed at the black and white wedding photograph of Eleanor and Artie as they danced. It was displayed on the wall next to a picture of Tina, Artie, and me at our wedding, studio portraits of Clare and Katy, and a sepia-toned photograph of Grandma Flora and Grandpa Willy.

A breeze from the overhead paddle fan ruffled the pages of a newspaper on the desk. It was my last copy of the *Sunday Essex County News*. Like Eleanor and Artie, I preferred to leave my Essex County days in the past. The pages flapped open to the obituary section and a headline caught my eye:

HOWARD SALTZMAN,

NOTED REDMOND ATTORNEY DEAD AT 80

Tina entered the room and held my arm. I shook my head and said, "He died on our tenth wedding anniversary."

"Strange," noted Tina. "I wonder how many others are out there, born of Saltzman's baby mill."

"We may never know," I replied.

I picked up a photograph of The Sisters, taken the day of Artie's funeral. How much my life had changed since that fateful day. "The Sisters knew Dory and Lana," I remarked.

Tina gave me a shocked look. "How do you know that?"

"Because I found Aunt Joanie's phone number in Lana McGovern's address book."

She gasped. "My God. Why didn't you tell me this before?"

"I didn't want to upset you with a new baby on the way.

"The Sisters were convinced that Eleanor ruined their brother's life by adopting me. Helping Dory and Lana was their twisted way of getting back at her. Aunt Peggy knew that Aunt Elizabeth would tell me about the adoption, and she alerted everyone involved."

I turned The Sisters' photograph over on the desktop.

"What happened to the pictures of Dory and Jim?" asked Tina.

"They're in a box in the basement," I replied. "Along with my adoption papers. I did keep one photograph close by." A small gilded frame hung on the wall with the snapshot of Eleanor holding me in her car outside of Redmond General Hospital.

Tina hugged me. "Everything will be all right now, Patrick."

Arm in arm, we exited the office to the sound of cheers and laughter. I turned for a last look at my parents' wedding photograph, and Eleanor and Artie beamed at me. Another vision appeared, but this time it wasn't a chilling vignette of vicious kidnappers. Instead, I watched a comforting motion picture of my parents as they danced across the ballroom to a Big Band rendition of "Sentimental Journey."

I smiled and closed the door behind me.

AFTERWORD

The authorities never launched an investigation
into the events surrounding my adoption.

Aunt Joanie and Aunt Peggy both passed away,
along with the rest of The Sisters. None of them ever
contacted me again.

Dory Sochek wasn't charged with any crimes.
Following the death of Howard Saltzman, Dory moved
into a home for the indigent and died in 2016.

I'm living a happy life with Tina, Clare, and Kate.

"I watched a comforting motion picture of my parents
as they danced across the ballroom to a
Big Band rendition of 'Sentimental Journey.'"

The last photograph of Eleanor and Artie.

Patrick with Katy, Clare and Tina.

ABOUT THE AUTHOR

PATRICK J. CALLAHAN is a writer, artist, musician, and songwriter. Born in northern New Jersey in 1956 and raised at the Jersey shore, Patrick produced his first original musical while in high school. He started *Eleanor Music Publishing* to showcase his songs, before opening Callahan Electric in 1987. Known as a talented caricaturist, Patrick's artwork was featured on a New Jersey TV34 "Dream Jobs" television segment.

At the age of forty, Patrick discovered a dark family secret and began an investigation into his unknown past. The incredible story that unfolded became the basis for his novel, *DECADES of DECEPTION*. He is writing a sequel to the novel, along with several other literary projects. His music CD, *American Original*, is currently in production.

Patrick J. Callahan is happily married with two daughters. He lives at the Jersey shore, and works as an electrical inspector.

52199625R00149

Made in the USA
Middletown, DE
17 November 2017